P9-CQG-282

SEABISCUIT

Ex-Library: Friends of
Lake County Public Library

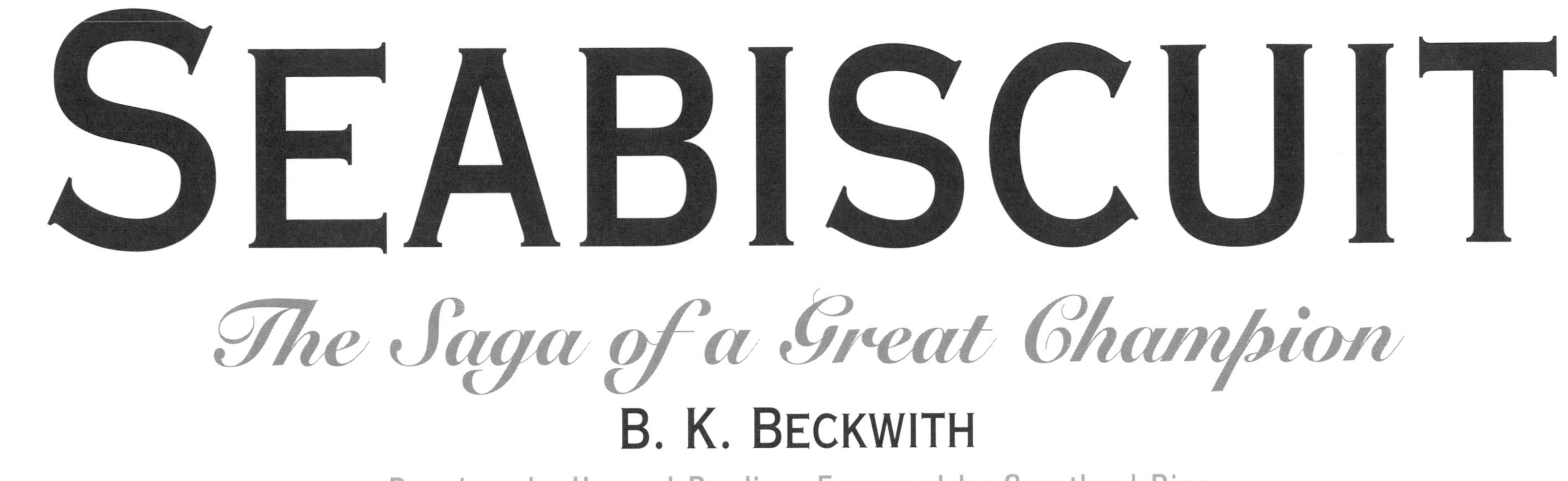

SEABISCUIT

The Saga of a Great Champion

B. K. BECKWITH

Drawings by Howard Brodie • Foreword by Grantland Rice

Westholme Publishing
Yardley, Pennsylvania

LAKE COUNTY PUBLIC LIBRARY

3 3113 02221 3534

"The Main issue in life is not the victory but the fight; the essential thing is not to have won but to have fought well"

Originally published by Wilfred Crowell, Inc. in 1940
Additional Material © 2003 Westholme Publishing, LLC
First Westholme paperback edition: July 2003

10 9 8 7 6 5 4 3 2

Westholme Publishing, LLC
Eight Harvey Avenue
Yardley, PA 19067

Submit book proposals in American, military, and sports history to the postal address above.
Material will not be returned unless accompanied by a SASE.

www.westholmepublishing.com

Library of Congress Cataloging-in-Publication Data
is available on file.

ISBN 1-59416-000-7

Cover design by John Hubbard
Picture Credits
4, 24, 29, 32, 35, 50, 54, 59, 62, 63,64, Carroll Photo Service; 8, 20, 42, Haase Photos; 12, Sutcliffe Pictures; 17, Tom Kelley; 46, Turf Pix, Morgan Photo Service, Morton & Co.
Frontispiece, Reproduction of an original painting of Seabiscuit by F. R. Voss
Printed in Canada

CONTENTS

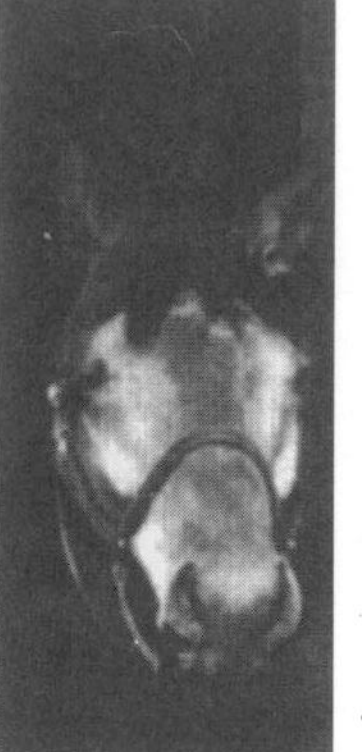

HERE IS a chunk of rawhide, surrounding a heart of iron, planked upon the four flying legs of a gazelle. Here is a combination of stretch thunder and wire lightning entered under the homely sobriquet of Seabiscuit, the horse that always gave you all he had, and often just a little bit more.

I saw him get the jump on the famed War Admiral at Pimlico in one of the great match races of all time. I saw War Admiral close up the gap and as they hit the head of the stretch, eye to eye, I could almost hear Seabiscuit say—"We're in the stretch now. This is where it counts. Let's see who can run."

I saw the game and gallant Biscuit break down at Santa Anita in 1939. I saw him limp from the track in the direction of a pasture—and racing oblivion. He was then six years old, a veteran whose flying feet had churned up dust from Texas to New England, from California to Florida, crossing the country from one ocean to another, moving from one box car to another in his transcontinental tour.

I saw him come from retirement in 1940 at Santa Anita, tackling one of the toughest slogans of sport—"They don't come back." And then from No Man's Land of racing, out from the mists and the fogs, the Mighty Atom from the equine world, proved the value of character and courage, the double value of heart and hoof. Seabiscuit came up the hard way. Grandson of Man O'War, he was never the pampered scion of a world renowned grandsire. To this fact I think he owes at least part of his greatness. The racing world left him on his own—and he accepted the challenge. Greatness was born within him. He had nothing exceptional to show on the outside. In this respect he was just another horse. He proved that while beauty may be only skin deep, the true greatness must reach the unfathomed soul.

The racing public that knew him, loved him I think, above any other horse that ever ran, not even barring Man O'War. He was one of the mob or crowd, no spectacular prancer that caught your eye. Man O'War was retired in his third year. Seabiscuit was retired in his sixth year and he still had enough left to set an all-time winning mark. Man O'War was never called upon to face the vital test of competition—"Can you come back?" Seabiscuit was. And it is here you get the true story of the most dramatic thoroughbred American racing has ever known.

There may be faster horses later on who will win more money. But there will never be a gamer horse—and I don't believe there will ever be another Seabiscuit. I think you will agree with me when you have read the story of his career.

Grantland Rice

Being the owner of Seabiscuit is an honor and privilege of which I am deeply appreciative. His courage, honesty and physical prowess definitely place him among the thoroughbred immortals of turf history. ¶ He has intelligence and understanding almost spiritual in quality and all of us who are close to 'Biscuit naturally have the deepest affection for him. ¶ The thrills he has given us will never be equaled unless one or more of his sons proves equal to the task of carrying on where the champion left off.

Charles S. Howard.

CHAPTER ONE «IT CAN'T BE DONE»

"IT can't be done," they said. All night before the race they said it . . . all manner of men . . . all over the world. . . . "It can't be done—they never come back."

They said it over gleaming dinner tables, in club rooms, in good motor cars, in beaneries and barrooms, in pubs and palaces, in the air and on the ground, by phone, by wire, by daylight and by dark. . . . "A great horse, sir—but champions don't come back."

Yet they kept their fingers crossed, and they prayed a bit, for they loved the old horse . . . so long now his gallant hoofbeats had drummed upon their hearts.

"It can't be done," said the taxi driver to his midnight fare. "I tell you it's askin' too much of him. High weight and a hard field. As I was sayin' to my missus. . . ."

"Laid up for nine months," interrupted the fare. "No—he's in too tough, even for him. But, by George, they'll know they've been in a horse race."

"Now take Dempsey or Jeffries," said the bartender as he polished a glass, "they couldn't make it—legs go, maybe a bit of the heart goes too. Champions don't. . . ."

They said it in crowded trollies and roaring subways; they said it over back fences in the long twilight; they argued over it in a million hotel lobbies that spanned the spinning earth.

"Ah come from old *Kain*tucky, myself," said the hotel cook to the second maid. "Me an that little hoss—a long way from home. I'd sho like to see him do it."

Standing in the darkness of a shed-row, looking into a lighted box stall, an angular, tight-lipped man said slowly:

"They'll see—he *can* do it."

Facing him, a little, hard, bay horse stood ankle deep in his straw bed, wide head hung forward, dozing. For the moment he seemed utterly unconcerned over the fact that on the morrow he would carry on his sturdy back the hopes and fears of countless thousands.

Tomorrow was another day. He would, as he had always done, tackle it when it came—face it with honesty and courage, and a great dignity.

The earth turned upward through the darkness, rolling toward the dawn of March the 2nd, 1940.

* * * *

A silver sword of daylight rent the mantle which draped the furrowed contours of the Sierra Madres. The black cloak slipped down from the mountain's crest, folding in shadowed pools at its feet.

The sword of light dipped and touched the granite of a Maltese Cross, saluting the last resting place of "Lucky" Baldwin's famous thoroughbreds. Beneath the Cross lay the bones of Emperor of Norfolk, Velante, Silver Cloud, and Rey el Santa Anita—horses whose glory had girded the globe. The sword, now brightening and glowing, moved from the immortal dead to touch, with the promise of immortality, the living.

The little bay horse stirred in his stall. The upper door of the box opened, the screen was thrown back, and the shaft flooded, momentarily, his sleep-filled eyes. Some message coursed down the beam . . . a message, perhaps, from those long dead . . . a drumming thunder from the paddocks of heaven . . . a bugle blowing from Valhalla . . . a challenge. . . . "Awake, little horse—it's your day! Let 'er roll!"

He shook himself. His body seemed to grow in size. The great muscles rippled under the gleaming bay hide. His fine head came up, the eyes deep and burning against the daylight which now flooded Santa Anita Park.

It was the morning of the Big Day. The world's richest race was to be run that afternoon . . . the Santa Anita Handicap . . . one hundred thousand dollars . . . one mile and one quarter . . . the gallop for gold and glory. . . .

Only, in the case of the little horse, so much more than that was at stake.

* * * *

Softly the stable came awake around Seabiscuit. Through the flat, clean smell of leather, the sweet aroma of hay, the faint pungency of liniment, came the sounds of men and horses moving about. Underneath the lulling surface, unmistakable to man and beast, lay a tension that was almost a tangible thing. . . .

"Today is the day!"

The horses sensed it and moved restlessly in their boxes, swinging their heads over the doors and looking down the shed-row to where the light shone around the old champion's stall. His head was clearly etched there, small ears up, the black bangs of his forelock sprayed across the wide, intelligent face. The crest of his neck was slightly arched. In that classic mold there was something of serenity, of assurance, and something of bulldog determination in the set of his broad jaws.

He alone showed no outward sign of the tension . . . but he knew he would race today.

Harry Bradshaw, his groom, came down the shed with a pail of oats. He poured them into the feed tub hanging by the door. The horse tossed his head with sudden impatience, stamped in the straw bed, nickered in short, insistent blasts. Food! No matter what the day, he could eat—and how! That ravenous appetite had been the bane of the stable for many a year. That sleek, hard barrel, ribs just showing, took as much thought and care as Milady's figure. How Bradshaw had watched it through those convalescent months at Ridgewood Ranch, fighting every excess pound against this very day!

"Easy there, Pappy—get back, you wolf." It was Harry's soft voice, his gentle hand shoving the old stallion's head away from the tub. "Yeah—you're going light today, Biscuit, m'boy—there's work to do—a hundred thousand dollars' worth. Three quarts of nice rolled oats—but that's all—no hay as a chaser." He set the bucket in the corner of the big double box. "There you are, champ."

The velvet muzzle whuffled deep in the feed. If he needed further proof that today was the day, this was it—three quarts, and no hay—and him as hungry and sharp as a she wolf! He sliced at the man with his teeth, but it was only in fun. It was a race day, and he knew it.

Harry went out and looked at the paling sky. It was here—March the 2nd—clear, and with a promise of warmth. After all these months bringing the horse back, the hour was almost upon them. Still looking upward into the dawn, Harry's lips moved. "Be with him today," he said.

Across the ring the tight-lipped man was walking, his face locked, his grey eyes, behind their heavy glasses, inscrutable, fixed on the stall door ahead. From him radiated the same sense of hooded power that came from the horse.

They are akin, these two—Tom Smith and Seabiscuit. Today is the climax of both their lives—the slow-spoken countryman, and the little bay thoroughbred. They have come a long way together, through victory and defeat, and today, whatever the outcome, they will share it in that strange communion which has made the man and the horse as one in the fulfilment of their destiny.

Smith moved slowly under the shed toward Seabiscuit's stall. His hand fooled with a piece of buckskin thong. Like David Harum, he works with a bit of tack, or whittles, while weighing his thoughts and his words.

Harry said, "He's right as rain, Mr. Smith."

A flicker of a smile lighted Tom's eyes. "Wrong word, Harry. Wouldn't need any rain today."

The groom laughed. "Don't worry—she'll be dry and fast out there." He jerked his head in the direction of the racetrack. "And you won't be able to pack the crowd in with a shoehorn," he added.

"Guess you're pretty near right." Smith stopped. "He's still eating. I'll wait."

But the horse had heard him, and now swung to the stall door. Tom went to him, studied him carefully for a long moment. He nodded slowly, and this time, though shared with no one but the Biscuit, his smile was broader. He touched the horse's splendid head with a strange gesture of finality.

"Today's the day," he said.

* * * *

Six, seven, eight, nine—the hours are marching—sentries of time—toward the great race. . . .

The Howard barn is all activity now, the even, pleasant activity of morning at a big racing stable. Fires are burning in the iron stoves on the ring, fragrant wood smoke filling the sunlit air. Sleek thoroughbreds are cooling out under their vivid blankets, others are held on lead shanks as they are "done up"—doused from head to foot, scraped with light aluminum bars, a liniment brace rubbed on over shoulder, back, and loins. Still others are being saddled to go out, pommel pads placed, exercise boys "thrown up," soft voices humming to flighty two-year-olds. Lead ponies wait patiently for the trainer or foreman who will take the "set." On the racetrack the beat of hoofs rises from breezing horses. . . .

Grooms are washing bandages, airing rub rags and night blankets, polishing leather, cleaning badger-haired brushes, shaking up and "setting the stalls fair," sprinkling lime deodorant, shining the brass name-plates on halters, sponging out eyes and nostrils, brushing out manes and tails, cleaning feet, removing the stall bandages and putting galloping ones on, scrubbing feed tubs, putting in fresh water and oat and timothy hay. Blankets and coolers are folded neatly beside the doors, temperature charts have been checked, the walking ring is kept raked and cleaned. Ancient and very polite dogs sit on their haunches and snap at flies they never catch.

The hours march on toward the sixth running of the Santa Anita Handicap. . . .

* * * *

The big boss came out at seven thirty—Charles Howard. Mrs. Howard came with him. Their faith in the old champion, and their love of him, had made this day possible. Against advice and criticism, against a million misplaced opinions, they had brought him back from retirement, knowing in their hearts that the third try at the world's richest race, the last try at Sun Beau's all-time money-winning record, must prove the charm.

In the short space of four years this horse had woven his personality into the pattern of their lives, so that now, what had started as a thread in the tapestry, was the major theme. They had lived close to his side, helping him and praying for him. They had watched his work-outs, weighed his worries, been heartened by his great heart. They had cheered his triumphs and wept at his defeats, they had trod with him every foot of his meteoric trail. from cast-off to king.

MAN O'WAR
TEA BISCUIT } HARD TACK →
Sire of
Seabiscuit

PROGENITORS OF A CHAMPION

← MAN O'WAR
Grand Sire
of Seabiscuit

← SWING ON { WHISK BROOM 2ND
BALANCE
Dam of
Seabiscuit

Seabiscuit was an honored and beloved member of the Howard family.

"The Howards are here," Tom Smith said to Harry. "We'll blow him out now." He turned toward the end of the shed-row. "Red," he called, "all set."

A slim, carrot-topped man, with a bow in his booted leg, a broad grin on his freckled face, and a blue eye as keen as the blade of a knife, came from the tack-room. He was part of this picture, too—a great part—Jockey Red Pollard, riding the comeback trail together with the horse that had made him.

Howard joined the two men. He shook hands with them, not as boss and owner, but as a friend stirred by the same deep emotion. He put his arm across the boy's shoulder and smiled down at him.

"How is it, Red?"

"O.K. Mr. Howard. Pappy and me will win today. We'll shut 'em out."

Tom Smith nodded at the ground. His faith was firm.

They went out to the track—Howard and Smith on their ponies—Red up on the Biscuit's back. Mrs. Howard followed to the racetrack rail. She had to grip it hard to keep her hands from shaking.

"Gallop him easy for a mile and a quarter," Smith told the jockey, "then break him off at the three-sixteenth pole and blow him out through the stretch."

The horse jogged away from them, reaching out, swinging his hooded head into the bit. He was beginning to feel the tension now—getting an edge—ready to run. Red stood high-poised in the stirrups, holding him back.

"Tom," Howard said, "he never looked better in his life."

"Never looked better, and never was better," the trainer answered. "That ankle is sound as a yearling's. His stride is freer, easier. The long lay-up did him good." He looked off at the huge, now empty, grandstand and clubhouse. "They'll see."

The Biscuit's tail lined out behind him as he gained momentum. His muscles rippled in shoulder and forearm, thigh and gaskin. One ear cocked back, listening.

"Easy, Pappy," the boy whispered. "This is just to get the feel of it."

The white rail of the track unraveled behind them.

* * * *

By air, by auto, by train, by trolley, by land and by sea—by the Lord Harry, they came this day to Southern California for the Santa Anita Handicap!

At nine o'clock in the morning all roads leading to Arcadia were packed with people. The vast parking area of the plant began filling in the early hours. Long lines formed outside the gates awaiting the opening. At eleven no seat in the grandstand or clubhouse was left, and the human stream was pouring out through the tunnel onto the lawns of the infield, eddying around the blazing beds of flowers.

And still they came . . . from nine to ninety, rich and poor, famous and infamous, plutocrats and pawnbrokers, bishops and bartenders, stars and stragglers, tycoons and toughs—good, bad, and indifferent—still they came, drawn to Santa Anita by a mutual and lasting bond—the love of great horses running in a great race. . . .

In this particular case, it was their love for one horse—a blocky little bulldog with an independent air.

Seventy-five thousand of them packed the place that afternoon, jammed it with color and excitement, and a great, throbbing expectancy. Seabiscuit would run . . . even now he was in the paddock, being saddled for the master effort of his life.

Tom Smith tests the girth, fastens the pommel pad, smooths down the cloth. Seabiscuit stands motionless in the saddling stall, head up, looking out over the crowd. He hardly sees them now. He is a bit bored, a bit insolent. The moment is almost upon him. The long tension of the day, of waiting through the morning and the early afternoon, is over. It had been a relief to leave the stable for the paddock. As always, he had been able to relax then, to save every ounce of energy for the race itself. His plodding, tired post parades had become famous. Under them lay a dangerous conservation of power.

Howard and Pollard are talking in low tones. Smith joins them.

"Take him out with Whichcee and Specify, Red," Tom says. "Get your position before the clubhouse turn—close up. Rate him down the backside. Make your move at the head of the stretch. You know him—shake him up when he needs it. Once on top, they'll never head you."

"Good luck, Red." Howard's hand is tight on the boy's shoulder.

The paddock judge comes down the line. "All set, Mr. Howard?" Charles nods. The judge raises his voice. "All right—take 'em out."

Seabiscuit, number one, leads off as they start up the runway toward the parade circle. The crowd surges close. Uniformed guards keep them back. "Make way! Watch out for the horses!"

Out from under the saddling shed comes the little bay horse. Applause runs down along the line of people. The sound rolls forward over the milling mass of humanity—echoing against the towering back of the grandstand. Seabiscuit stops for a moment, as though in recognition of the tribute. A bystander breaks past the guards, tries to touch the horse. He stands quietly—well-mannered but aloof.

The horses move on to the parade circle. The waves of sound spread outward, swelling. White rails are black with people. The field circles the ring. Owners and trainers and jockeys are huddled on the lawn—last orders given in hushed voices. Heelfly rolls a wicked eye, War Plumage, the filly, is in a lather, Don Mike is the picture horse, Whichcee and Specify fidget, Kayak II, the rangy long-limbed giant, paws the earth, Seabiscuit nods at the cheering crowd—the others are strung out behind, waiting.

"Go to your horses." The judge's voice raps the command. "Riders up!"

There is a vivid flash of color against the sky as the jockeys are given a leg up, their silks flaring. Headed by the red-coated pony boy the thoroughbreds file toward the racetrack. As the old champion steps out on the course the cheering rises into a bedlam of sound. Below the clubhouse the horses turn and start back, and all along the line of the parade the vast throngs rise, hats off, shouting, yelling, applauding. Santa Anita has never seen a day to equal this one—few racetracks have. It is the most remarkable demonstration ever accorded a racehorse going to the post.

Pollard sits still on his back, reins loose. Quietly he marches up the stretch toward the gate. A few moments longer and he is in the starting stall, looking down the course.

All those racing years of his life, then, are culminated in this. Down the course ahead lies the final answer to whatever he has done. The up-hill trail ends here . . . eighty-eight races run, fifty thousand miles of railroading, a dozen track records, good going and bad, victory and defeat, War Admiral, Stagehand, Rosemont, and the others . . . the entire picture fades now and leaves but the one course—the mile and one-quarter ahead. . . .

The roar of the crowd dies . . . seventy-five thousand people hold their breaths. They are waiting for the rolling thunder of hoofs. . . . "There they go!"

CHAPTER TWO «SWAYING ON SPINDLY LEGS»

"THE sun shines bright on my old Kentucky home. . . ."
The stable hand hummed it as he walked down the lane toward the foaling barn. He had heard them sing it first, right here, seventy years ago—the white folks singing from the great veranda on the hill one moonlit night. He stopped now and leaned on a fence rail. Through the blue-green fields below him mares browsed, their gangling foals at their sides. Occasionally one of the youngsters galloped off on brittle legs, the mother plodding patiently behind, swishing at flies. A set of twins argued over the suckling privileges. Some of the babies near the fence heard his soft voice—"the young folks roll on the little cabin floor. . . ." They moved, ever curious, ears up, tiny damp muzzles out, toward him.

"The sun shines bright . . ." a May sun in old Kentucky. It flickered on the waters of a stream, flashed above on the white pillars of the big house, filtered through the trees to glint on the shiny coats of thoroughbreds. The stable hand stopped singing, sighed, rolled his tired eyes at the foaling barn, and shuffled off again.

"Noah!" He looked up, quickened his step. Down the lane ahead a man was riding toward him on a white horse.

"Yes suh, Mister Hancock—I'se comin'."

Arthur Hancock, master of mighty Claiborne, heritage of fine horses, reined close and looked down at the white, crinkly head of the old man.

"Did they bring in Gravita and Flambino and White Favor?" he asked.

"Yes, Mister Arthur, suh—they's in yonder. Reckon their time is powerful close."

Arthur Hancock sat his white horse thinking that it was Flambino, mated with Gallant Fox, who had produced Omaha. Not yet to the races, that one looked full of promise. And now she was heavy with another Gallant Fox foal. The red fox of Belair might well prove one of the greatest progenitors ever to grace the lovely acres of Claiborne. And Gravita, too—exquisitely molded Gravita—she was in foal to Gallant Fox, and her time was almost upon her. White Favor he had bred to Diavolo. The result of that should prove interesting. So deeply and hopefully he thought of these three that he scarcely heard Noah's voice:

"That young Whiskbroom mare, Swing On—she done drop her colt, suh," Noah said. "Runty lookin' little fella," he added.

Hancock moved in the saddle. "Swing On, eh—that'll be a Hard Tack colt. Let's have a look at him, Noah."

He was up at his mother's side when they came to the stall door. He wabbled a bit on his legs, turned, and regarded them. "Maybe I am a runt," he seemed to say, "but I'm not afraid of you."

"Independent looking little cuss," mused Hancock. "Nice, honest eye—and what there is of him is clean and well-set."

"Don't have any resemblance to any of 'em, do he, suh," Noah said. "Not Hard Tack, nor his grandpappy, Man O'War—nor even his mammy."

Seabiscuit—though he had no name at the moment, other than runt—swayed again on his spindly legs, caught his balance quickly, and continued to stare at them. He could not see beyond them over the lower half of the stall door—he could not see the rolling reaches of Claiborne, nor the green fields of Bourbon County, nor the dizzy heights of glory to which he would one day climb.

No more could Hancock and Noah see, encased in that midget mold of horseflesh standing before them, the tiny, growing flame of greatness.

They turned away, Hancock's thoughts again busy with the approaching confinement of Gravita and Flambino and White Favor. Behind them the little colt stamped his foot and went to nursing diligently. It couldn't have been vibrations in the soil of Claiborne—a faint, challenging thunder—which caused Gallant Fox and Sir Galahad and the rest of them to pause momentarily in their stallion runs, ears up, listening? . . . No, not from that tiny foot—yet pause they did. . . .

* * * *

He grew of course, but not very fast. It was only the dominant quality of his head that would have made you stop and look again as he wandered with his mother in the rich pastures of Claiborne. But the chances are ten to one you'd have been too busy looking at Gravita's son, Granville, or Flares, who ran at Flambino's side, to even notice the wide-eyed runt. And then there was White Favor's foal, White Cockade, and the sleek looking Snark, and others—all in that famous 1933 crop—who drew the eyes of horsemen more than little Seabiscuit, son of Hard Tack and Swing On.

To be sure his owners, Mrs. Henry Carnegie Phipps, and her statesman-financier brother, Ogden Mills, who planned to race him under their nom de course of Wheatley Stable, came to see him, and no doubt they expressed some enthusiasm. They may have remarked that, though he appeared to be a trifle sprung forward, he had a good blocky look to him, a nice hind leg, and splendid quarters. He was deep in the girth, too, and close-coupled, his head well set on a fine neck which tapered gracefully into a nicely sloped shoulder. Oh, he had quality, but the package was so small that it was wrapped in, and you couldn't see beneath the bay hide how big the heart was. You could look into those eyes, perhaps, and read it, but that's not easy to do in a paddock stocked with so many splendid youngsters.

How could the Wheatley people know that he would carry their yellow and purple silks forty-six times before ever he really came into his own? And then only under other silks—the western red and white of the Howards. Over half his races run before he found his true stride—and it's a wonder then those iron limbs would even carry him! They had too many horses, those other people, and Sunny Jim Fitzsimmons, the grand old man of racing, needs must give his eye and his thoughts to the Granvilles and the Omahas, and those who showed the early promise.

You must not blame them too much—those who knew him "way back when." Racing is a keenly competitive game, and big stables must concentrate on the "likely ones" of the moment. Feed bills run high! Today Sunny Jim is the first one to admit that Seabiscuit fooled him, and, grand sportsman that he is, the loudest to sing his praises.

The truth is, the key to this remarkable horse's greatness lay in the hands of but two men—Charles S. Howard and Tom Smith—and they did not come out of the West to unlock his dazzling speed until he had raced more times than is recorded in the average horse's lifetime.

So they looked over the paddock fence at Claiborne—all those other people who now hardly seem a part of his life—and they saw Granville, Flares, Snark, White Cockade, and a host of horses, whose hoofprints in the racing sands of time are but little marks alongside the seal of the son of Swing On.

S E A B I S C U I T

How did he get his name? From his sire and granddam—Hard Tack and Tea Biscuit. It is, of course, the obvious derivation. His mother, Swing On, seems to have little connection with him in this one respect. Grandma and pop were responsible for the rather unwieldy handle of Seabiscuit. It was quite a load of letters for a young colt to carry around. In spite of which, it was to become a household word in every state in the nation.

Tea Biscuit, who had once raced in England in the colors of her breeder, August Belmont, was purchased in foal to Man O'War. The result of that union was Hard Tack. Judge C. J. FitzGerald, dean of American racing officials, who was years later to preside over Seabiscuit's greatest triumph, bought the mare for James Cox Brady for twenty-five thousand dollars. She was later sold to the Wheatley Stable with her young Man O'War colt by her side. That youngster, Hard Tack, through his sire and dam, carried a potent double strain of the great imported horse, Rock Sand, winner of the English Derby. Hard Tack himself, a slashing big fella, was never much of a racehorse, having bowed a tendon in 1930 before he had a proper chance to prove his real worth. He was sent to Towson, Maryland, to stand his first season at stud. The following year he was moved to the Blue Grass Heights Farm of Howard Davis, which is located near Lexington, Kentucky.

MR. AND MRS.
CHARLES S. HOWARD

It was here that Swing On was bred to him, being returned to Claiborne to foal. Both sire and dam were but seven years of age, the very prime of life, when their illustrious son was born. Hard Tack, thanks to the greatness of that son, now stands at Claiborne.

Perhaps Swing On had little enough to do with Seabiscuit's name, but it is certain that the royal blood of such as Ben Brush, St. Simon, and Meddler, which flowed in her veins, had a lot to do with his racing prowess. If she said anything to him there in the fields of Bourbon County it was probably, "Keep out of the way of those big boys—eat and grow, and bide your time. That time will come, little son."

He must have gotten the general idea, for he was a self-contained, methodical little cuss, even then. Or perhaps he sensed the future more than anyone.

* * * *

The time passed rapidly there at Claiborne. Before you knew it he was no longer a suckling, but a weanling, on his own in a very big world. And then fall rolled over the farm into winter, January 1st of 1934 arrived, and he was a full-fledged yearling, bright bay in color with perfect black points, still small, but compact and quick on his feet.

He was taken up with the others and gentled, familiarized with the many things humans would do for him, and with him, through future years. He was halter broken and taught to lead, to stand tied in a stall, to grow accustomed to human hands and a gentle pressure on his back. It was a very gradual process, a very easy one, this learning adherence to man's rules. He schooled readily enough, and though at times his definite mind indicated stubbornness, it was found that once he fully understood what was expected of him, he did it with good grace. This quality of dignified good manners was to grow on him through life. Given the opportunity to relax he was, and is, more capable of doing so than the average thoroughbred. That must have come from his dam, because neither Hard Tack, nor the majority of the House of Hastings, have minded their manners too well. Seabiscuit holds all of their vital fire, but controls it like the great gentleman he is.

In August of 1934 he left Claiborne forever. Gone were the carefree days of childhood, days of rollicking in green fields, galloping free with the other colts, skimming under the big trees, browsing by the river, swishing flies, sleeping in the sun. He was off to Aqueduct now, the Queens County course—off to meet Sunny Jim Fitzsimmons, to meet the feel of a saddle and the weight of a jockey, to learn to stand in the starting gate, to break with the others, to breeze through the stretch, to feel that strange, magnetic communication of kindly hands coming down the leather of a rein, to go through long hours of "legging up" and "fining down," to have sore and tender shins—to learn, in a word, not to run—a knowledge and love of which had been born and bred in him—but, as must all green colts, to race.

A few short months now and he would be a two-year-old. The railroad car rumbled northward and eastward toward New York, and toward the fulfilment of his destiny.

CHAPTER THREE «THE FUNNY LITTLE HORSE»

On January 19th of 1935, with the flamingoes sprayed in a pink fan around the infield lake, and the palm trees drooping like vast umbrellas, a likely looking field of two-year-olds walked from the paddock at Hialeah Park. Most of them were a bit skittish, eyeing the crowd, and sidling and prancing in the post parade. Few people paid more than passing attention to the squarish bay colt who walked onto the track with rather a short, choppy stride and a definitely serious air about him for one so young. No one had, or could have had, the remotest idea that he or she was watching the curtain rise on the most remarkable drama ever to be played on the American Turf.

A young lady leaning on the rail said, "Oh, look at the funny little bay horse—he looks tired already."

Regardless of which, the curtain rose, and the play began—a bit slowly to be sure. The "babies" were lined up and in a moment were off, winging and swerving down the three-eighths of a mile straightaway.

Seabiscuit came fourth. Biblically that might mean something. On the chart it meant simply that, starting from an outside post position, overcoming mild interference following the break, he had turned in a creditable, though hardly brilliant, effort.

To his entourage it was probably reasonably satisfactory. It's a cinch it wasn't very impressive, for two days later, when the "set" came out on the racetrack for the morning gallop, he was still demurely last, and least, in the line. Their decision that he was not top-flight material could hardly have been arrived at that early—none the less, the decision came to pass. He was, in the not too far distant future, to be typed as a good, sturdy "overnight" and minor stake performer. As a matter of fact he ran for claiming prices as low as twenty-five hundred dollars; which means that this price was all his owner considered him to be worth at this time. You or I might have bought a half million dollars' worth of horseflesh for less than three thousand! He seems to have been tabbed as the sort of colt who will start once, sometimes twice a week, and help take care of the general overhead of a big stable. His knees looked a bit doubtful from the beginning, growing into what is known as "popped," the left one all his life more sprung than the right. The rest of him was made of iron. He would do, but he was no White Cockade in Fitzsimmons' eyes, nor even a Snark.

The year and a half that Sunny Jim had him he also trained Omaha, champion three-year-old of 1935, and Granville, who came along to be top three-year-old of 1936. Small wonder that the runt got overlooked.

So the race meant not too much to the stable, and little or nothing to the patrons of Hialeah Park on that January day.

However, we must, in all justice to this great drama unfolding, pause here a moment and take true account of what it meant to the future.

Seabiscuit is a horse of records—fourteen track records, records at four and five for money won by any horse of corresponding age in two consecutive years, a world's money-winning record, a traveling record, a national and international publicity record, a comeback record—but that day in Florida began the most astounding record of his, or any great horse's, career.

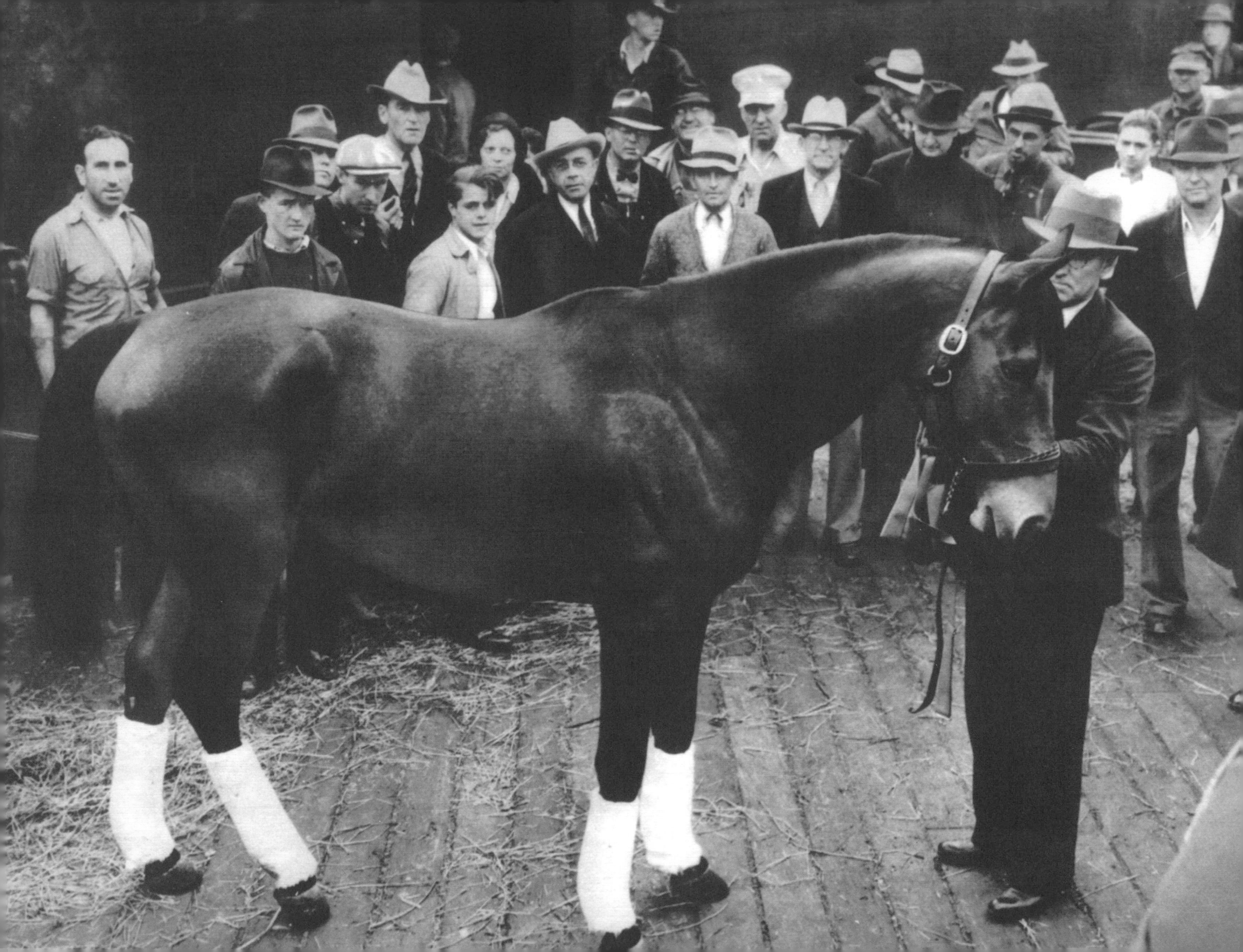

No claim is made that two-year-olds have never been raced as many times as this horse. But the claim is definitely made that no two-year-old, who later went on to become one of the greatest horses of this, or any other era, ever raced thirty-five times at that juvenile and formative age. It is one of the miracles of racing history. It must, and does, speak volumes for the heart of Seabiscuit. Consider that, beaten thirty times in that first year, he yet went on with bulldog courage, overcoming physical defects and mental hurdles, to eventually become monarch of all he surveyed. Of such stuff as this is greatness made. Among horses, perhaps among people, there is no parallel.

To record those thirty-five races would be useless. He ran them, and they stand on the books for anyone to read, but somehow, other than what they proved of his durability in mind and body, they are not a part of this story.

True, a glimmer of his real self showed on occasions—he won the Watch Hill Claiming Stakes at Narragansett, running the five furlongs in 59 and 3/5, breaking the track record—he won the Springhill Handicap at Agawan, and the Ardsley at Aqueduct, and two other overnight events. But he had started seventeen times before ever he entered the charmed circle—ten of those starts before May the first.

George Woolf, who rode him in October at Suffolk Downs, said that his disposition was souring then from the long grind. "He went up in the air with me at the start, and was generally mean, restive, and ragged," George told me.

He ended that first gruelling year, unfound, but for what he knew lay within himself, waiting for one man to discover. He had won $12,510—5 firsts, 7 seconds, 5 thirds, 18 times unplaced. He ran his last 1935 race on November 11th at Pimlico, having opened the campaign on January 19th. The charts had given him credit for coming from behind and closing fast. They hadn't mentioned the fact—since charts don't—that he wasn't yet satisfied with himself, or anyone else, that, in all honesty, he was doing his best to find himself—and that his poor knees ached, and, at the end, he was just plain "bone tired."

CHAPTER FOUR « A HUNCH ABOUT A HORSE »

"That bay there, Seabiscuit," Fitzsimmons said to his assistant, George Tappen, "I haven't figured him out. Been too busy with some of the others, I guess. He's got something, George."

"He's got early lick from the gate," Tappen answered, "when he wants to show it."

"I know. Ever since the day he came from the farm, he's been like that—got something when he wants to show it. He's too docile, too quiet—almost like he's got an inferiority complex. Half the time you might mistake him for a lead pony."

Tappen laughed. "He certainly conserves his energy. Remember how hard he was to work in the mornings?"

"Yes," Mr. Fitz answered, "I do. And that loafing in the morning got him to loafing in the afternoon. He's too prone right today to let horses come to him—to be on top and get sociable, and just wait for the others. It's a dangerous habit."

"That's why you raced him so much as a two-year-old, isn't it, Mr. Fitz?" Tappen asked. "I mean, because he wouldn't work in the mornings?"

"One reason. The other was because I knew he would take care of himself. He's wise as an owl, that little fella. You notice how he lies down in the afternoons after his meals? Saving himself—but for what? Pretty soon we've got to find out, George, or quit worrying about him."

Fitzsimmons snapped his stop-watch as the chunky colt broke off at the three-quarter pole. Still with his eyes on the running horse, the old man said, "Even those bucked knees—they may bother him, but he can travel like the wind on 'em when he chooses to."

"Look now," George Tappen points up the stretch at the colt, "see how they splay his front feet. Those bum knees make him paddle like a darn duck."

"He's movin' this morning—flattens out, drops his head and levels that tail when he's in a hurry—and when he's alone and not waiting for other horses." Fitzsimmons pressed the watch again, glanced down. "Thirteen flat," he said. "Not bad, but he's not really working for us yet."

Sunny Jim was right—the colt had not found himself. It was a bad period in his life—the kind that all of us must go through at one time or another. He had grown careless and lazy in this early part of his three-year-old season. He was young and discouraged, and a bit bewildered. The road ahead seemed a dark, endless tunnel. Where did it lead? Where was the light? Fitzsimmons could not give him all his time—there were Granville, Snark, White Cockade, and a host of others. He could only help whenever possible, and hope that the little bay horse would find his way through. Somehow, he believed he would. He knew what was there—courage and honesty and brains, and a bulldog will. It was just growing pains he was having, like any youngster. He would snap out of them, but until he did—well, he was definitely second-flight material.

Young horses, like young people, form habits very easily, both good ones and bad ones. That trick of letting horses come up to him while running, loafing a bit, was, as Mr. Fitz had said, a

dangerous and costly one. It took a deal of curing—actually, it had to be watched, in less and less degrees, all his racing life. It was the reason you saw him shaken up with the bat at the head of the stretch in many of his races. He was on top, you remember, both ears cocked forward, careless of any sound behind, coasting. And when the boy clucked to him, or cut him a couple with the whip, you saw that right ear drop back, listening for other horses, ready then to look 'em in the eye, kill 'em off, and go on. Tom Smith used to cut a hole in the back of his blinkers so that the threatening shadow could be seen before it was too late.

Gradually he overcame this youthful fault, but there was one occasion, prior to the cutting of the eye hole, when the realization of danger did come too late—the 1937 Santa Anita Handicap—Seabiscuit's first try at the world's richest race. A length on top and a hundred yards from the wire—he couldn't miss—but both ears were pricked, and Rosemont was coming on the outside like a hurricane. The Foxcatcher Flyer nipped him right at the wire, too late to shake him up, and beat him the width of the back of your hand.

They learned—Pollard and the rest of his riders—never to ease off on him too soon. Keep clucking to him, talking to him, and he'd run all day for you with his lion's heart, but Smith and Howard often enough held their breaths until they saw that one ear back and one ear forward, and knew he was listening and ready for any challenge.

Understand that if a horse did get up to him, shake Seabiscuit up, call on him at any stage of the race, and he'd go on with his rival forever—bulldog him to death. As a matter of fact, his ability to "look 'em in the eye" caused him to virtually break the heart of every horse he worked with in later years.

Oh, he was human. He had his little mental quirks which had to be ironed out. Who hasn't? No one can ever question his courage, nor the honesty of his running. The records give undying proof of those qualities. This trick merely came from a habit formed in youth which he did not properly understand, and which took the individual patience and care of a Tom Smith to set right.

Let it be said here and now that, during this formative period of his life, Seabiscuit was never used by Jim Fitzsimmons as a work horse for the great Granville. True, that has become the popular conception through the years, but it is a myth builded upon fancy.

"I would not then, nor would I now, ever take a horse from one division of my training establishment and assign him as a work horse for a colt from another division. Seabiscuit was owned by the Wheatley, and Granville by the Belair." That is Mr. Fitz's own statement, and in it the Dean of American trainers definitely refutes the "work horse" theory.

Granville, we know, went on to become the horse of the year, but we are not interested in that. We're interested in the year 1936 as it affected Seabiscuit. It turned out to be, when more than half over, a very momentous one for the little bay horse.

* * * *

Racing had been revived in California in 1934. Sportsmen throughout the Golden State recalled the heyday of Haggin's and Baldwin's glory, and they sought to emulate these men. Great horses would be bred in California again—this they felt certain of, and are now proving—but first it was necessary to journey eastward that the stock might be looked over, purchased where possible, and brought to the Pacific slope, both for racing and breeding.

One of the men most interested in these two pro-

jects was Charles Stewart Howard, San Francisco sportsman, automobile magnate, and ranchman. He had a few horses in his barn that ran average sort of races. George Giannini had sent him a man called Tom Smith, ex-cattle rancher, bronco buster, rodeo rider, blacksmith, trainer, and general all-around horseman.

"This fellow knows more about horses," Giannini told Howard, "than any dozen men. Why, Charlie, he goes clear back to the time when he used to break 'em for the Boer War. He went to a professional horse-breaking school in Texas when he was thirteen. He's been around 'em ever since, and he's done everything there is to do with every kind of horse that ever looked through a bridle."

That was a pretty fair sort of recommendation. Added to that, both men were born in Georgia. Smith went to work for Howard. He's been at it ever since.

The two of them decided at Tanforan that spring that they'd ship the stable east, race a few, and look around.

"This game is on the rise out here in California," said Howard. "I like it—it's a grand sport and a healthy one. The horses we've got are fair, Tom—but I want the best."

"A good horse," said Tom laconically. "We'll do the rest with him."

They were a potent combination, those two, when they wanted something. And it was a great day in the morning for Seabiscuit when they rolled over the Rockies, eastward bound.

It won't be long now, little horse. . . . You're coming into your own. . . .

* * * *

"He looked right down his nose at me," Tom Smith said, "like he was saying, 'Who the devil are you?' What did I do? Why, I just stared right back at him. I liked his looks. Reminded me of some darn handy cowponies I've seen."

That momentous meeting—if such it can be called, for the rail of the racetrack divided the two gentlemen—occurred on the 29th of June, 1936, at Suffolk Downs outside of Boston. Little or no wind blew to relieve the oppressive summer air. The gentleman from California stood on the clubhouse ramp, and the gentleman from old Kentucky had stopped momentarily in the post parade, perhaps disturbed by the analytical glance of the Westerner. Neither knew it then—in fact Tom will admit that he didn't think much more about it until a month later at Saratoga—yet history was in the making.

The colt jogged off after the pony boy, and Smith had his first view of a robust rump that was to become the focus of many a spent horse and desperate rider.

"Rear view, front view, all around—he kind of struck my fancy," Smith said. "No, I didn't know his name. I checked on my program for that—Seabiscuit, three-year-old, good breeding. Well, we were looking for that kind, if they could show anything. He showed me quite a lot. They were going three quarters. He got away a bit slowly—acted up at the gate—down the backside he lay eighth, then moved up to sixth on the far turn, and headin' for home he started running over horses. He won going away by a length and a half in 1:11 and 4/5, packing 115 pounds. Deliberate and Liberal came one two behind him, I remember. He picked those horses up nicely. He was pounds the best. When he came back to the stand I nodded at him. Darned if he didn't nod back, kinda like he was paying me an honor to notice me. 'I'll see you again,' I said."

He did. But not until Saratoga. Charles Howard was there, and the Westerners were getting ready to deal their cards.

* * * *

Saratoga in August . . . the mecca of horsemen . . . shimmering heat and elm-shaded streets, pillared hotels and wide verandas, crowded bars and barber shops, ancient hacks and dusty coachmen, gleaming motor cars and country houses packed with guests, horses being saddled under the vast trees of the paddock, jostling good-natured crowds, coats in the clubhouse, shirt sleeves in the old wooden stands, the lovely informal course, and the jumps on the infield. . . . Saratoga in August . . . racing by day and dining and wining by night, workouts in the warm dawn and sales in the evening . . . memories flooding back through liquid twilights . . . seventy-five years of racing . . . Gallant Fox, Equipoise, Sun Beau, Discovery, Man O'War, Exterminator, Roamer, Beldame, Parole, Tom Ochiltree, Harry Bassett, Longfellow, Preakness, Kentucky —the galloping greats of other years marching through the tunnels of Saratoga trees, their hoofbeats a muffled thunder heard 'round the world. . . . Saratoga in August. . . .

* * * *

The third day of the meeting Charles Howard sat in his box at Saratoga. The horses were coming out on the track for the running of the Mohawk Claiming Stakes. He had just arrived from California—in fact, he and Mrs. Howard had come directly from their hotel to the course. He glanced at his wife and wondered how the deuce she could look so cool in this heat.

"Remember," he said, "we're in the market for a good horse."

"It's too late now," she answered, "but you could have claimed any one of these. What do you think of them?"

He studied the post parade. "What about that little bay—the blocky one with the black points running clear up his legs?"

She looked at the colt's number and checked on the program. "Seabiscuit," she said, "owned by the Wheatley Stable. I'll bet you a cool drink he doesn't win it."

He took the bet and in a moment the horses were off. Seabiscuit won by six open lengths, on top from flag-fall to finish. To be frank, he made a holy show of his field.

Howard laughed. "Come on," he said, "I want a long, deep lemonade." And, half to himself, as they moved away—"Think of it—in there for six thousand dollars! Unless I'm much mistaken that one will bear looking into."

They had the lemonade. It represented the only bet Mrs. Howard ever made on Seabiscuit.

Later, in the paddock, they met Charlie Strub and Webb Everett, on from Santa Anita.

"If you're looking for a good horse," Webb said, "that Wheatley colt has all the ear-marks."

"I was thinking the same thing myself, Webb," Howard answered. "It's a wonder to me that he wasn't claimed out of that race."

"I've an idea they'd put a price on him," Strub said.

The picture of the little bay stuck in Howard's mind. "I'll get hold of Tom Smith," he told his wife. "We'll look him over, and then, if I like him, I'll see Ogden Mills. I'm pretty sure we can come to some agreement."

"Don't wait too long," she cautioned. "I'd hate to lose him—I've got a sudden hunch about that horse, even if I did lose a bet on him."

Meanwhile Seabiscuit ate his three square a day, stall-walked at night, and remained oblivious to his great destiny.

Tom Smith went over and sounded out Jim Fitzsimmons.

"I don't know," Sunny Jim told him, "this horse has been raced a lot, but he's just beginning to win for me. That's my business—having winners in the barn. I'm not anxious to part with him now, but if Mr. Mills says O.K. I won't stand in the way of any deal."

Smith looked the horse over. "I told you," he said, "that we'd meet again." And to Howard he reported: "I remember him from that day at Suffolk Downs. I liked him then, and I still do. He's run down, thin, and his knees are bucked. Better come and see him yourself."

Howard went back to the Wheatley barn with Tom. The colt was led out. He swung his fine, sane head at the San Franciscan and gave him a shove with his nose. His left knee was dangerously sprung.

"That won't necessarily stop him," Tom said. "We'd have to go along easy with him, feel him out, build him up."

Howard, quite honestly, fell in love with him.

"I can't describe the feeling," he told me the other day, "but I knew he had what it takes. And Tom knew it, too. He wouldn't say much then—he naturally wanted me to decide—but I don't think he was ever in too much doubt about the horse from that day to this. We had our worries and troubles ahead. We had to rebuild part of him, both mentally and physically, but you don't have to rebuild the heart when it's already there, big as all out-doors."

To Smith he said, "The rest is up to Mills."

It took two days for Ogden Mills to make up his mind. Howard had offered $8,000 for the colt.

"I'd let him go," he said, "but the women of the family have grown kind of fond of the little fellow."

Forty-eight hours later in the paddock Howard asked: "Well, deal or no deal?" And Mills answered, thinking, if the horse were going, he was glad it was to California, "Deal."

Forty-seven races run, and now his real life was to begin . . . the soil of twenty-five different racetracks to unravel beneath the wizardry of his flying feet, rocketing him to record after record, until at last the long trail ended high against the blazing light of immortality.

CHAPTER FIVE «PUMPKIN»

The feed tubs and the stall doors and the blankets—they were all red and white now instead of yellow and purple. And the man who was around him most was unhurried and soft-spoken. There was something strangely akin in this man, and from him radiated a steady, purposeful strength, the aura of which eddied about the horse. Oh, he didn't relax at once, he still walked at night in his stall, he was irritable. The change would take time, but he felt Smith's power, and he sensed the potent resolve of the man whose firmness and kindliness were to guide him over the rough spots ahead.

The very first day in the Howard barn he met Pumpkin. The big, placid palamino lead pony intrigued him from the start, and that liking grew into the first real friendship he had ever had with another animal. He had never disliked anyone, he had tried to be courteous, but a certain reserve of manner had been born in him—a shyness, perhaps, due to his size. Those big youngsters in the paddocks of Claiborne had just run over him, or kicked him out of their way. And since leaving there he'd never had time to make friends.

Pumpkin, in his turn, took a shine to the little stranger. The newcomer, he figured, was doing his best to pretend he was a snob, but he looked all in. The golden pony towered over him, then reached down and stuck his muzzle against Seabiscuit's. The latter nipped at him in momentary annoyance, but Pumpkin didn't draw away or bite back. Seabiscuit gave him the once over, decided it wasn't freshness but friendliness, and whuffled.

Tom Smith, standing with his right leg splayed out till the toe of his boot wobbled at right angles to his body, nodded approvingly. He snapped his knife shut, and tossed the whittling stick away.

"Put the pony in the stall next to Biscuit," he said, "and cut a window between 'em. We'll let 'em do a little visitin' back and forth."

They've been "visitin' back and forth" ever since. The Western horse probably told him about California, and years on the range, roping cattle, and standing quiet in a branding pen when calves were raising the devil all around you—saving your strength and your nerves for the big moments. "You thoroughbreds are all alike," the palamino might have said. "You think because your family goes back four hundred years that you can act like prima donnas. Look, little fella, my family goes back more than four hundred years. We first came into California with the Conquistadores of Spain, and we were old then. We've learned to take it easy, and do our work. Those two fellows, Howard and Smith, are all right. You work for them and they'll work for you."

It was an odd twist of fate that Pumpkin, who had helped Seabiscuit to relax, to gain weight in those early days, was, for that very reason, not allowed to accompany him when he came out of retirement years later. The champion had come to lean too much upon his old friend, and for that 1940 campaign, with pounds of excess flesh to whittle away, there must be no lolling in the lead pony's unhurried atmosphere.

Smith started galloping Seabiscuit for a few days on the work track at Saratoga—feeling him out. He'd get himself into a lather

THE "GREAT TRAVELER" DISEMBARKS

every time he was saddled. They began taking him out with Pumpkin, and he calmed down a bit, but was still track weary and fed up.

"He lugs in badly," Tom told Howard, "and I don't like that trick of loafing with other horses."

"How about the knees?" Howard asked.

A half smile curved Tom's lips. "I've got a little mixture—a liniment I worked out thirty years ago—it'll help with 'em. Still, we'll have to go easy. We can't train him like other horses—can't work him as much. Right now that don't bother me. I want to let up on him, get some flesh on those bones."

Howard patted the horse's strong neck. "It's up to you, Tom. Get acquainted with him in your own way. Let him know there's nothing for him to worry about. We'll ship to Detroit in a few days and give him his first airing in our silks out there." He paused. "Unless, of course, you want to throw him out of training for the rest of the season."

"No—time enough for a let up when we get back to California. Got to run him a bit first to find out what the kinks are."

Three days later the stable entrained for Detroit, and they had their first real eye-opener as to just how bad his nerves were. When he got to the loading platform he broke out in a dripping sweat. It poured in rivulets from his belly and down off his heels. He refused to enter the car at first. Good old Pumpkin, placidly plodding, was brought up, and with a bit of persuasion Seabiscuit followed him into the steel-ribbed inclosure. They gave him the entire end of the car—a space usually allotted to three horses—and the lead pony was put opposite. Pumpkin made himself comfortable at once, half dozing in the heat. Seabiscuit, weaving restlessly, watched him. The older horse nibbled aimlessly at a piece of his bedding, got a delightfully long wisp of straw, and letting it dangle from his mouth, went back to dozing. Occasionally it started to slip out, and he opened one eye, flapped his lips, and caught it. The racehorse stopped weaving, became fascinated, his eyes glued on Pumpkin.

A whistle hooted up forward, the train jerked, and then slid away from the platform, gaining momentum. The first leg of the fifty thousand miles of railroading that lay ahead, was begun. Saratoga dwindled down the rails behind until it was only a blur in the summer haze. Strangely enough, he was never to race there again.

Stranger still, following that bad beginning he was to become the most perfect, the most blasé traveler in thoroughbred history. Pumpkin had a lot to do with that. As long as the old pony occupied the royal drawing-room with him he was perfectly happy.

"Once," Tom Smith told me, "I had to wake him when we arrived at Pimlico after a trans-continental trip. Sound asleep and not too anxious to get off."

Another time—it was at Del Mar and he was loading to go East for the great match race with War Admiral—Smith and I followed the horse and Pumpkin into the car. Overhead navy pursuit planes were roaring up from the near-by airport. They were skimming the top of the horse pullman so close you could have whacked them with a broom, their motors gunned wide open in a deafening racket. Seabiscuit never even flicked an ear. He went on board, looked around, nodded at the palamino pony as much as to say, "This seems adequate," and, before the train was moving, lay down for a snooze.

* * * *

He showed them several things at Detroit, the most important of which was burning, dazzling speed. They had Exhibit, a better than average sprinter, and one morning, just to get a line on Seabiscuit, they worked the two horses together. Exhibit tried to stick it for three-eighths, had all he could stand, folded like a tent, and was never the same horse afterwards. He was the first of a long line to choke on the same medicine.

The Motor City Handicap, run on August 22nd, saw him answering the bugle for the first time in the famous red and white triangle silks, and it also marked the first appearance of a horse and rider combination which became the toast of the sporting world. In the stirrups that day was Jockey Jack Red Pollard, and he would stay in them for the next twenty-five starts the Howard champion made.

In those twenty-five races Seabiscuit and Pollard, competing in the top stakes and handicaps of the country, were destined to enter the winner's circle sixteen times, run second twice—both nose defeats in track record time—five times third, and only out of the money on two occasions.

Yes sir—those were Red Pollard's stirrups, and they would stay so until a broken collar bone and a broken leg put the boy on the shelf for almost two years. However, it was Cougar Red who was to come back from retirement with Seabiscuit and prove that combination a winning one in their greatest triumph. But that was three and a half years later.

In the Motor City the colt ran fourth. He went out on the early pace with Myrtlewood, fastest mare of her time, and then was eased back by Pollard for a breather. That was a mistake. The rest of the field came to him, and his loafing trick cost him many lengths. Turning into the stretch he had but one horse beaten. Red went to the whip. Oh—so it wasn't all over, eh? Sorry—my fault. He came on again like an express train. Both the jockey and the horse had had their first lesson. Pollard knew why he had lost it, and he knew he had been aboard a whirlwind. He went to Charles Howard directly after the race.

"Mr. Howard," he said, "that's going to be a great horse. He's the next winner of the Santa Anita Handicap—you mark my words."

Howard smiled into the boy's eager, excited blue eyes. "If that's the case," he answered, "I guess we ought to have a red-head on his back."

"Can I ride him?"

"From here in," Howard said.

That's the only deal they ever made, and Red Pollard is still wearing the red and white silks.

* * * *

Charles and Mrs. Howard were both at Detroit on September the 7th to see their racing colors come home in front for the first time aboard the flying back of Seabiscuit. It was a sight to be repeated before their eyes many times, but one which never failed to bring them cheering to their feet with the thundering glory of its repetition.

Making one of his famous stretch drives the little bay colt caught Professor Paul at the wire, with the grand Irish-bred "leppin'" horse, Azucar, getting up for third money. Seabiscuit gave Professor Paul ten pounds, and six pounds to Azucar under the scale. He ran the mile and one-eighth of this race, The Governor's Handicap, in 1:50 and 4/5. It was an impressive performance, and he came out of it in good shape.

At the end of the Detroit meeting he scored again, this time by four lengths, carrying top weight of the field in the Hendrie Handicap, one and one-sixteenth miles in 1:44 and 2/5. He won in a common canter, and there could be no question now about the Howards hav-

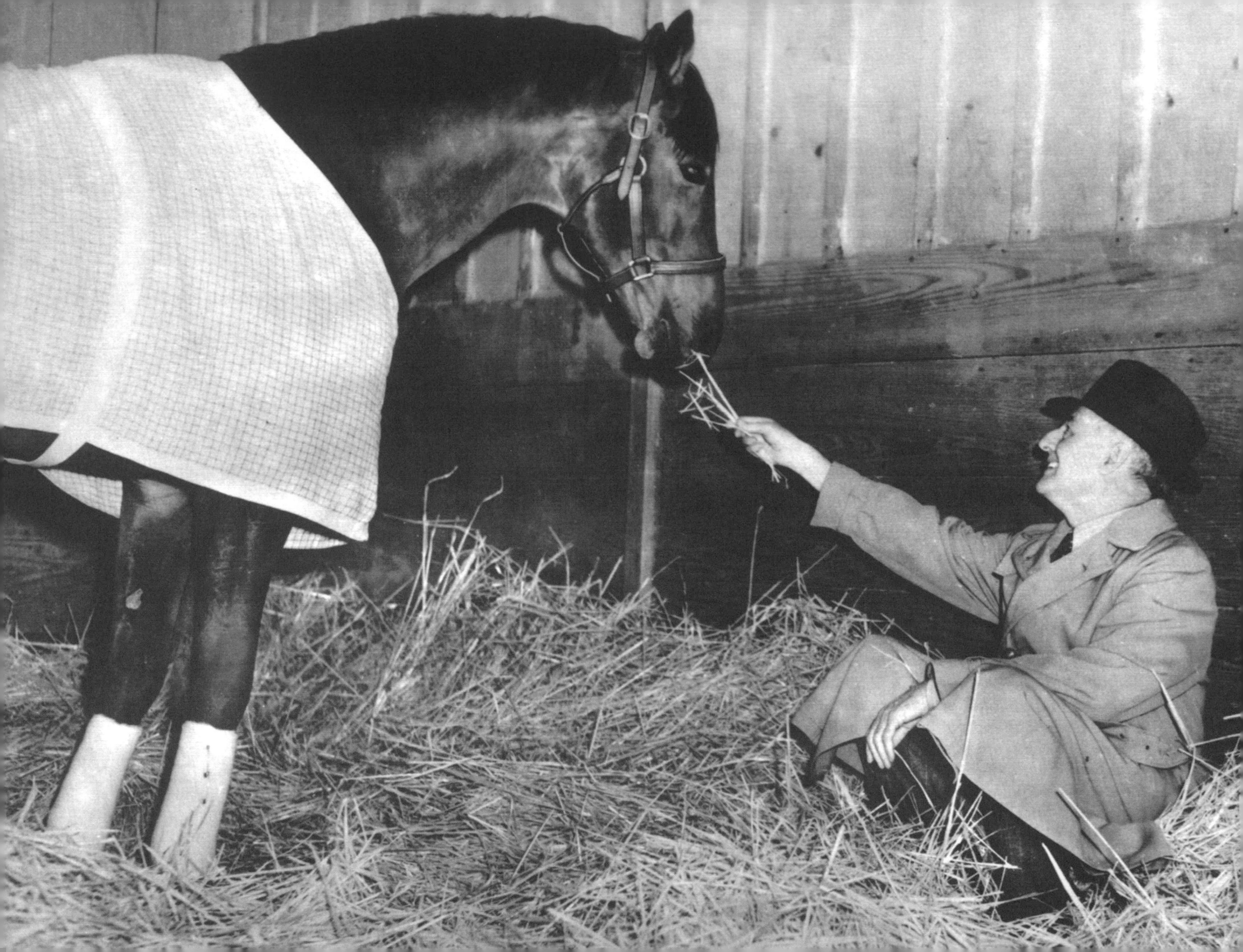

ing "A good thing"—just how good no one knew. Certainly he was getting more kindly in his work, and he was looking better—some of that needed two hundred pounds was beginning to round out the rough spots. He did not lug in to the rail as badly, though his post manners were not perfection yet.

They went to River Downs at Cincinnati where he got two thirds in his only two starts. He was making big weight concessions, even at this early date. The next move was eastward again to Empire City where, on October 24th, he took the Scarsdale Handicap, again coming from way back to win over Jesting and Piccolo by a neck. Already—just two and one half months after his eight thousand dollar purchase—he had, as the saying goes, "won himself out."

His eastern farewell for 1936 came in the Yorktown Handicap. Loaded with top weight of 119 pounds he came very fast in the stretch, but could do no better than third.

"Let's head for California," Howard said to Tom Smith after the race. "A little wind off San Francisco Bay will do us all good."

"Yes," Tom agreed, "it's what the doctor ordered. He's been racing now since the middle of April. We'll give him a breather."

So they rolled out of Empire, homeward bound.

"We're coming back," Howard told them, "and when we do, hang on to your hats!"

A good piece of advice, as it turned out.

* * * *

"California, here I come!"

They'd have had a brass band out to meet him that day at Tanforan if they had known how grandly his mark was to shine in their sun. From the moment he first set foot on California soil, he was to become the little Westerner . . . he was to gallop his way into the hearts of his adopted state until today he ranks among her foremost citizens, and her proudest possessions. The personality of the horse was such that to all people, be they in high places or lowly ones, he was, and is, both friend and champion.

Through the years to come he was to carry the banner of California to the four corners of the earth, reaching, by the mediums of the press, motion pictures, radio, and word of mouth, to places where he could not go himself. In one year alone he received more newspaper space than Roosevelt, Mussolini, or Hitler!

He was, because of his exploits, to become one of the great factors in bringing the thoroughbred horse back to California. He was, largely in himself, to be the principal focus for hundreds of thousands of tourists. In a word, he became news from Pekin to Paris, from Argentina to Alaska, and, though born in Kentucky, he carried the stamp of California upon him from that long gone November day when he walked from his car at Tanforan and first breathed the crisp air blowing in from San Francisco Bay.

What did he possess that made him so much a part of our lives? It cannot be aptly defined—words are a poor medium at best. . . . Quality, if you wish . . . the innate poise of a great gentleman—the divine simplicity of a great soul . . . magnificence both in victory and defeat . . . the throbbing pulse of winged beauty that caught at our hearts and dimmed our eyes. . . .

No, you can't define it—whatever it is that holds us. Perhaps it is something we see in him that, in a small measure, we like to think we possess ourselves. . . .

* * * *

That air from San Francisco Bay had the right tang to it—no question about that. However, the local chamber of commerce couldn't claim everything, for, in the next two weeks, Seabiscuit proved to his entourage that, constitutionally, he was something of a freak. They had thought it might take some time to bring him up to his peak condition, but in short order it became evident that he needed only a few days to accomplish what the average horse would take months to do.

He gained weight, he quieted down, he went back to work and loved it, and, in no time at all, he was rarin' to go to the races again. Smith had schooled him every morning at the gate, making him learn patience, making him stand quietly waiting for that bell.

"I just got in front of him with a light stick," Tom told me, "and tapped him across the chest and shoulders. Never too hard, but enough so that he knew I meant business. You got to go at a horse slowly teaching him most anything. Easy, firm repetition does it. He caught on quick enough—he's wise as an old owl."

They were racing down the peninsula at Bay Meadows. The Howards began to thumb through the condition book. The horse was getting sharp as a tack, so why not run him.

"How about the Bay Bridge Handicap on November 28th, Tom?" Howard asked. "It's at a flat mile."

"Fine," Tom agreed, "he'll be ready."

He didn't tell Howard then that the horse would be a "mortal lock" in the race. He didn't tell anyone—sometimes he hardly dared whisper it to himself. "It's a fact," he said, "he was getting so good he scared me. I'd never seen the kind of speed he was showing in his works. He burned the top off the racetrack."

They vanned down the ten miles to Bay Meadows for the Bay Bridge race. He had top weight of the field—116 pounds. It was his California debut—and what a coming-out party! Before the race they were sitting on their hands, wondering and watching. After it was over they were screaming their heads off!

Completely left at the post, Seabiscuit started out after his field. He seemed to fairly swallow the ribbon of the racetrack, picking up and passing horses with such ridiculous and overpowering ease as to make them appear anchored. Pollard could have stopped to read the afternoon paper in the stretch, and still won. He cantered home, ears pricked and counting the customers, five lengths on top. They hung up the time—1:36 flat, a new track record.

Time is taken when the flag falls. Official clockers of this race naturally pressed their stopwatches when the first horse out of the starting gate passed the flagman, and he dropped his red cloth. However, two old-time clockers have since told me that they had their watches on Seabiscuit alone in this Bay Bridge Handicap, and that the Howard color-bearer was a full second behind the others when he left the post. Their watches both agreed that the horse covered the mile route—and eased up at the finish, remember—in 1:35.

This is cited, purely unofficially, to give some idea of the phenomenal speed possessed by Seabiscuit. Assuming that these two clockers were correct, it is one of the fastest miles ever run. More than that, had the horse been pressed at the finish it is likely that a new world's record would have been recorded that memorable afternoon.

In any case, Seabiscuit was on his winging way . . . and all California was yelling as—well, as only Californians can yell when they get their hearts into it. . . .

Next on his schedule came the World's Fair Handicap, ten thousand dollars, one mile and three-sixteenths, to be decided at Bay Meadows on December the 12th. Did he have it at his mercy, or not? Some said yes and some said no. There were older horses running for this juicy prize, some pretty fair eastern handicap campaigners like Infantry, Giant Killer, Tick On, and Noble Count. The little three-year-old son of Hard Tack had yet to prove himself with that kind. And would he go the distance? Mustn't go overboard on him too soon, reasoned the wise ones.

They might as well have jumped off the deep end and held their breaths. Seabiscuit ran them all dizzy—the other horses and the patrons! Off well this time, he put away the favored Infantry in the first half mile, drew out to a margin of eight lengths going down the backside, coasted around the far turn, letting the groggy pack come to within four lengths of him, and then cantered down the home stretch to win as he pleased by five. He hung out another track record of 1:55 and 4/5—just 4/5 off Discovery's world record—and when he came back to the winner's circle he wasn't breathing hard enough to blow the suds off a stein of beer!

The year 1936 was closing, but the gateway to glory was just opening for the little bay horse. From April to December he had galloped his way from New York to San Francisco. He had started twenty-three times in this three-year-old campaign, earning $28,995, most of that in the last few months under the Howard banner. He had won nine races—six of them stake and handicap events—been second once, five times third, eight times unplaced.

Little did he, or any of those about him, realize that there was approximately $400,000 worth of running yet to be done!

CHAPTER SIX «ROSEMONT—SEABISCUIT»

Santa Anita—the Colossus of Arcadia. . . . Out Huntington Drive, the Biscuit's pullman rolled under a warm winter sun, and he walked from the car onto the long platform the most talked of horse in the United States. Understand, he was still the great question mark in the minds of most people. The human race is hard to convince, and, though the winter book operators had already made him favorite for the Santa Anita Handicap, there was many an eastern eyebrow lifted. Whom had he beaten? And here, where the great ones came seeking the pot of gold, consider those he would have to beat. Top Row was here, and Time Supply, Rosemont and Red Rain, Indian Broom and Mr. Bones, and others who loomed large in the national picture. It was a long order for a horse that, less than a year ago, had run with a $6,000 claiming tag on him!

One wonders, as he followed Pumpkin down the platform under the speculative eyes of newsmen and eastern trainers, if he could have had any realization of the fact that here, in the purple shadow of the Sierra Madres, he was to experience the greatest emotions of his life . . . that here, beaten twice for the world's richest race by nose decisions, later broken down on this same track and branded as through, he was yet to come back from his retirement in the pine-clad hills of Ridgewood, and win the race he had thrice been denied.

It was here he was to enact the final scene in the most remarkable of all racing dramas, and at this course he was at long last to reach his goal of world's money-winning record holder. It was here, through his superb qualities in defeat more than in victory, that he was to become both a national idol, and a very human little guy.

Well, of course, he didn't know anything about this as yet. All he did know on this first arrival day in Arcadia was that his skin bothered him no end, and he was, worse luck, breaking out with lumps on him as large as the end of your thumb. In fact, even Pumpkin couldn't quiet him down, and he took to stall walking again in earnest.

They got him a goat—a nice whiskered old chap, guaranteed to relax anything. Often goats serve this purpose with high-strung thoroughbreds. They sleep in the stall with 'em and, one way or another, take their minds off their troubles. Unfortunately, in this case, the goat's manners concerning food were not of the best. One afternoon, without even a by-your-leave, he moved Seabiscuit away from his dinner. The latter had never been known, worried or otherwise, to miss a meal, and he had no intention of beginning now. He did not do anything about it at first. He was kindly at heart, and besides he rather liked the goat. He stood off and thought it over, then made another try at the groceries. Mr. Goat got tough and Mr. Biscuit got mad. For the first time in his life he completely lost his temper. He picked old whiskers up by the scruff of his back, and shook him like a terrier shakes a rat. Then he heaved him under the screen and out of the stall—out, I might add, for good. What might have been a beautiful friendship, ceased.

"The skin trouble was bad," Tom said, "and it held us up on him longer than I've ever cared to admit before. It undid a lot of work. We had to scratch him out of all those early stakes that winter, and work him back slowly to his peak."

And they had other troubles, too. In spite of his recurrence of nerves he continued to take on weight. For two reasons he could not be worked sufficiently to keep that avoirdupois down—one, the skin rash, and the other, his tricky knees. They were never entirely sound throughout his racing life. They were painted with Tom's own pet liniment and wrapped at night, but he could not be drilled on them too often.

"The clockers used to think I was hiding him out on 'em," Smith said, "working him by moonlight." He laughed. "Most of the time I just wasn't working him. He's always come up to a race with less preparation than the average horse—he's had to. That's why we used other methods to keep his weight down—those rubber-lined hoods—breezes in the afternoon when we fooled him, let him think he was going to the races and sweat and worry about it all day. I didn't make a habit of fooling clockers intentionally. I guess I just got the reputation."

They watched his diet day and night. It wasn't long before he was having to wear a muzzle, sometimes twenty-two hours out of the twenty-four. He'd eat his bedding without it. The truth is, Tom watched everything about him, continually and with meticulous care. It is doubtful if any human ever received such well-balanced, measured attention. Many a night the trainer never left the stable, and this was not from any undue worry about the horse. Tom Smith just felt better there, and it's certain the horse felt better knowing he was there. They understood each other, these two.

* * * *

On February the 9th he answered the bugle for the first time in 1937, and also made his first appearance at Santa Anita Park. It was the Huntington Beach Handicap, to be run over the seven furlong route. The huge course was packed to the rafters that day, for Rosemont and Time Supply would contest the issue with him. What would the bay colt do in company of this calibre?

Nothing—other than to show them a very nice pair of clean and fancy heels, a streamlined rump, and a flattened out tail. He won, back in the bridle, by four and one-half lengths. Sir Emerson was second, Time Supply third, and Rosemont out of the money. Even the easterners sat up and took notice. Where had this little package of dynamite been hiding?

The San Antonio Handicap came next. It was to be his last out before the $100,000 Santa Anita, which now was but one week away. Sixteen horses went to the post. The start was rough, and he was shuffled back, being fourteenth going into the clubhouse turn. From there on he was carried wide, and the crowds, who had made him favorite, could only groan and pray. It didn't do any good. He ran around horses at the far turn, and closed strongly, but could do no better than fifth.

This was to mark the only time he ran out of the money during 1937. More than that, there was to be only one similar occasion during the rest of his racing life.

* * * *

February 27th, and sixty thousand people flooded the magnificent grounds of Santa Anita Park for the third running of the world's richest horse race. Eighteen of the country's crack handicap stars paraded postward, with Rosemont, the Foxcatcher Flyer, favorite, the Baroni entry of Star Shadow and Goldeneye second choice, and Seabiscuit and Time Sup-

ply, each at approximately six to one, third in the selection of the bettors.

The huge field was away well. Seabiscuit, breaking from number three post position, was shuffled back by the early speed horses, and lay ninth passing the stands the first time. Special Agent and Boxthorn were setting a frightful pace—the first quarter in 22 and 2/5, the half in 45 and 4/5. At this point Pollard moved his horse, and the bay fairly flew at the leaders. From ninth to fourth he thundered. Ahead lay Special Agent, Boxthorn, and the giant California-bred colt, Don Roberto. Time Supply and Rosemont were still far back, but picking up horses steadily. Into the far turn Boxthorn was through, Don Roberto was wabbling. Seabiscuit passed them like an express train, and now only Special Agent galloped between him and the wire. Turning for home against the deafening roar of the crowd the little Howard horse went to the front. He seemed to be drawing away. Special Agent was done. At the sixteenth pole the Biscuit's ears were pricked. Was it over?

No, by the Lord Harry—a long way from that! In heaven's name, Pollard, if he's got anything left, shake him up! Does the boy feel that hurricane coming behind him? Rosemont—flying on the outside—running as few horses have ever run through the stretch before or since. . . . A frenzy of sound rolls out at the two horses. Richards on Rosemont is riding like a demon, his whip lashing. Pollard is sitting still. Inch by inch the big red horse gains. They're twenty feet from the wire—fifteen—ten—still Seabiscuit has it—has it by half a length—a neck—a head. They're at the wire—locked together. . . .

A gasping, shivering silence hangs over the vast crowd. Who got it—Seabiscuit? Rosemont? No one knows. The minutes waiting for the picture seem like hours. Charles Howard stands white and tense on the racetrack. Dick Handlen, trainer of Rosemont, stares at the ground, hands clenched. Tom Smith is motionless. There is a whir from above as the picture shoots down from the camera booth atop the stand. The judges are studying it now. How long—how long! Suddenly the numbers flash on the board across the track. It is Rosemont—Rosemont the winner—by a nose!

Howard stares at the board a moment, then smiles. It's a tough job to get out that rather sad looking grin, but he does. He walks over to Handlen. "Congratulations, Dick. It was a great race, and the best horse won."

That point has been argued ever since wherever horsemen gather. Nothing must be taken away from Rosemont. He gave on that day a superhuman effort, a magnificent exhibition of courage and speed. However, it was felt then, and it still is today by a majority of experts, that, had Seabiscuit been shaken up a hundred yards from the wire, he would have been the victor and not the vanquished.

It is history now. Perhaps, in the light of subsequent events, it is just as well for the little horse that this history was written as it was. . . .

CHAPTER SEVEN «HANG ON TO YOUR HATS»

LET her roll, little hoss, let her roll . . . your time has come. . . . Come it had—and roll he did—from racetrack to racetrack, from record to record. Seven straight he took now, and all who dared to face him were left in the explosions of dust which rose from beneath his flying feet. Relentless and irresistible he went on his thundering way, and those who had doubted came to cheer, and those who had lifted their eyebrows now lifted their hats. The little runt of Claiborne, the Wheatley cast-off, had found himself. And what a find it was!

Closing day at Santa Anita he took the San Juan Capistrano, seven lengths on top, high weight—which from now on he was always to carry—a new track record for the mile and one-eighth of 1:48 and 4/5, laughing at his field. San Francisco again, and this time the town turned out by the thousands. The triumphal march was on. The Marchbank and the Bay Meadows Handicaps were next, and he left the racing strips smoking from the touch of his plates in those brilliant victories.

Howard had said, "When we come back, hang on to your hats!" Well, they were on their way now, rolling eastward with the road-bed beating a challenge. New York was still doubtful of the little westerner. They couldn't forget his two and three-year-old seasons—more often, they couldn't remember just what he had done. He'd have to show 'em.

He did.

"If we take the Brooklyn," Tom said, "we're set. Aneroid is in that race, and he's coming off wins in the Metropolitan and the Suburban."

It was the east against the west—Aneroid against Seabiscuit. The last quarter of a mile they ding-donged it together, running as a team, but the Biscuit out-gamed him and won by a nose. Rosemont was in the ruck—nowhere. Revenge was sweet. Was he the best horse in America, then? Could he have climbed from obscurity to the heights in so short a time? They were beginning to think so . . . only a little more proof. . . .

He gave them plenty.

"We went down to Empire for the Butler Handicap," Howard told me, "and it was so hot you couldn't breathe. We'd come from California, where it was cool. We were plenty worried, but it didn't seem to faze him. He was made of iron. Somehow you knew to look at him that he was going to go on, that nothing would stop him—weight, distance, anything. He's been able to give us that kind of assurance often enough when things looked toughest. How? I couldn't tell you—it's inside him."

In the afternoon at Empire they'd take him outside under a tree, and four men would fan him with cloths, trying to give him some relief from the heat. They'd have done better to have fanned themselves—he was all right.

The handicappers were getting their heads together now. What would check him? The weight had been going up on him steadily—120, 122, 124. They gave him 126 for the Butler, and Pollard booted him to the wire an easy winner, one-fifth of a second off the track record. He had been badly fouled in this race—for which the offending rider was set down by the stewards—and he came out of it with a dangerous looking cut just below the left front ankle—the same left front where two years later he was to rupture his suspensory ligament.

It didn't stop him then—nothing could have. He won the Yonkers by four lengths, packing 129 pounds and breaking a track record which had stood for twenty years. The reverberations from that shook the country. The easterners were convinced. Here was a great horse. They took him to their hearts. He had ripped through the heat of a New York summer and cooled out all those who had ever doubted him.

Six straight victories. . . . Where next? . . .

They marched on Boston—Suffolk Downs—the very track where Tom had first seen him one year before. The Massachusetts Handicap, $50,000, the richest prize of the eastern summer season, was up for decision on August 7th. He had been assigned the staggering impost of 130 pounds for this classic. Few horses have won great handicaps carrying anything above this weight, and yet it is recorded that loud were the "beefs" when this pound allotment first became known. Why, they were practically giving him the race! What was the handicapper thinking of?

What a reversal of public opinion a few short months had brought about. And what a grand tribute to a grand horse.

The pick of the entire country met him that day. He gave them from two to thirty pounds, and a sound beating into the bargain. He galloped to a new track record of 1:49 flat, and he earned for owner Howard the tidy sum of $51,780. He was climbing up that money ladder fast, but, more important, he was now recognized beyond any shadow of doubt as the handicap champion of the nation.

Leaving Boston he went to Saratoga to bask in its sunshine and his own reflected glory. He was not seen under colors there. It was felt he needed a breather and his owner and trainer decided not to run him again until September 11th, when the $25,000 Narragansett Special would be run at the Rhode Island course.

In the meantime he continued his gallops and took unto himself an odd, flop-eared pup as stable companion. The dog was certainly of very doubtful origin, small, woebegone, and most pathetic. No one knows just why the horse asked him in and said stay as long as you like. Perhaps, now that he was king, he remembered the lonely cast-off days, the friendless yearling, and his big heart went out to this little dog. Pocatell, the pup's name was, after Pocatello, Idaho. He'd sit in a chair by the stall door during the daytime, sleeping with one eye closed and the other open, and woe to any stranger who came nosing around the Biscuit's domain. And at night he slept inside the stall.

Talk of a match race between Seabiscuit and War Admiral, grandson and son of the peerless Man O'War, was started at this time. War Admiral dominated his three-year-old division as completely as did Seabiscuit the older horses. Which one was the better? The arguments were long and heated, and the press of the nation took up the clamor. It would be a natural—the race of the century. It was a natural, and certainly one of the great sporting events of all time, but it was not destined to take place for another year. Meanwhile the pot of public conjecture simmered, sides were taken, sore spots rubbed, and various citizens went out on verbal limbs to wait with growing impatience for either Seabiscuit or War Admiral to saw them off.

At Narragansett it rained—how it rained! The track became a sea of mud and slop. Would he go, or wouldn't he? He went, with 132 pounds up, giving huge chunks of weight to the others lined up against him. The poundage and the slippery going took their toll. Grimly he splashed his way down the stretch to finish third behind Calumet Dick and Snark. He never gave up for a moment, and was only beaten two and one-half lengths.

Reams have been written about Seabiscuit and muddy tracks. It has been pretty generally recognized that he was far from his best on "off" going. He won over tracks labeled no better than "good"—in fact the official chart for the 1937 Santa Anita Handicap, when Rosemont nipped him a nose, was called "good." However, in the few times that he attempted "mud" or "slow" he obviously did not like it, and did not win. In these few cases he did, of course, carry top weight, and heavy loads are not helpful to a horse's footing under such adverse conditions. Then again, some horses are born "mudders," and others never acquire the knack. One thing should be definitely corrected, the statement that he couldn't stand up in the stuff. Once reaching his peak condition, he never ran worse than third in the mud.

"He'd just made up his mind that he didn't like it," Tom Smith said, "and he's got a pretty definite mind. Alone, he could work well on the worst kind of a track, but when it splattered in his face, and particularly in his ears, he wanted no part of it. Oh, he'd go on, try—he wouldn't have quit in a Wyoming hail storm where they come down as big as golf balls—but he couldn't, somehow, give his best—and why punish him unnecessarily. And another thing, don't forget we had to watch those knees pretty close."

So they kept him out of the mud wherever possible—for his sake, and for the sake of that vast multitude who loved him.

Four more times he went postward in 1937. Back at Jamaica he won the Continental by five lengths, 130 in the boot; next came the Laurel Stakes in Maryland in which he dead-heated Heelfly for first place; then on to Pimlico for the Riggs Handicap, where he triumphed by a neck in a superb drive with Burning Star, giving the latter 16 pounds, and hanging out a new track record for the mile and three-sixteenths of 1:57 and 2/5.

His last race of the year was on November 11th in the mile and five-eighths of the Bowie Handicap .To beat him it was necessary to record a new Pimlico record for the distance, and this the fine mare, Esposa, did, coming to the finish a thin nose on top—Seabiscuit 130 up, Esposa 115. It was grandly run by both of them.

And now the stands empty, the "captains and the kings depart," and the racing wars are over for 1937. The red and white blanket is thrown over his shoulders and he is led up the racetrack. He is not a tired horse—his head is high and the fire in his eyes is undimmed—but "he shall rest, and faith he shall need it."

Fifteen times he has answered the bugle as a four-year-old, ten different tracks have seen him, thousands of miles of railroads have rolled beneath him—he has met them all and given quarter to none. In those fifteen starts he has won eleven, come second twice —both nose defeats—been once third and once unplaced. He has earned $168,580, which places him at the top of the year's money winners, War Admiral having dueled with him for that honor.

He is the new king of the turf, but it hasn't turned his head. There is a bit more dignity in that carriage, perhaps—a maturity ripened with conquest and stamped with greatness. But there is nothing obvious about him, or gaudy. He is conscious of the limelight, and he likes it—the click of a camera has a definite meaning now, and he poses for pictures with a polite but pleased reserve. Glamour has grown about him—he is already a legend—but it is the "rags to riches" legend of the simple, honest soul. Royal blood flows in his veins, but it is warm blood. He has "walked with kings, nor lost the common touch."

And perhaps, after all, that is the answer. . . .

CHAPTER EIGHT «STAGEHAND BY TWO AND ONE-HALF INCHES»

Some things we try to do in life seem "jinxed" for us. Usually they are the big things, the most important ones, and because of that, if we have the fight and the courage, we grit our teeth and keep on trying. The "breaks" can't run against one always, and somehow, we keep telling ourselves, if we honestly persevere the goal will be won.

And yet in sports, where the months and years must, of necessity, take their toll, the goal becomes more and more difficult with the passage of time. To the average individual, as the old joints stiffen up and the pins get sore, it becomes impossible. Only the mind and the heart carry on. Yet this they will do and, on occasions, make that "impossible" take back for the word "possible". In the very rare instance the "possible" becomes an actuality. It takes intestinal fortitude to go on climbing when the heights seem insurmountable, and it takes that extra last ounce of fight which is the reason for a champion.

"Did you ever see two stallions fight?" Tom Smith asked me one day. "They look about evenly matched—most times they are—but one of 'em has that last reserve of courage and energy which licks the other. Seabiscuit has it."

The greatest fight he had in his life, the thing which, more than anything else, makes him stand out above his contemporaries, is the Santa Anita Handicap. I don't mean the running of this great race in any one year—I mean his long and gallant fight to win it.

We come, now, to his second attempt in this California classic—the 1938 running. One week prior to its decision he went postward—his first start since the Bowie at Pimlico—in the San Antonio Handicap. Temporary retirement had already come to one-half of the famous racing team, for Red Pollard was in the hospital nursing a broken collar bone. Sonny Workman was up that day. Giving a grand account of himself, and 12 pounds to the victor, Seabiscuit was beaten a nose by his old rival, Aneroid. The race was impressive. In no way did it detract from his role of favorite for the big handicap one week hence. When that day came it found him parading under 130 pounds, and carrying the bulk of public money at slightly less than two to one. He was California's darling—bring on your easterners. . . .

In that field, burdened by the feather of 100 pounds, there was a strapping young three-year-old called Stagehand—a colt who went on to become champion of his division for 1938. He had, two weeks before, won the Santa Anita Derby, clearly demonstrating his class, and his phenomenal stretch running ability. As they lined up at the post there were many of the wise ones who shook their heads. Could the older horse give this youngster 30 pounds and a beating?

George Woolf rode the Biscuit that day—George "the iceman," subbing for his pal Red Pollard. The latter, brought from the hospital, was on the roof of the grandstand, shaken and white and praying. Mrs. Howard was also high atop the stands, standing near Clem McCarthy, who was to broadcast the race to a waiting world. Charles Howard and Tom Smith sat in the Howard box, and neither of them spoke a word or saw anything save the little bay horse.

Seabiscuit was in number 12 post position. At the break the

horse on the outside of him came over sharply and all but knocked him to his knees. Woolf was thrown far forward, but stayed on him. The crowd groaned. Was he out of it? Not the Biscuit! They swept by the stands the first time and he was lying far back in the pack, seemingly hopelessly blocked off by a maelstrom of flying feet. Down the back stretch Woolf saw an opening. I've got to take it, he reasoned, or I'll never get clear. Who can blame him then in the heat and roar of the moment. It was now or never, as he saw it. In the light of later events we know, and he has said as much himself, that he should not have moved with the horse so soon. But he did, and the record is written.

The next half mile, from the ¾ pole to the ¼ pole, Seabiscuit was caught by private clockers in 44 and 1/5 seconds. Consider that this was in the middle, approximately, of a mile and one-quarter race, and consider also that the listed half-mile world's record is 46 and 1/5! Those two facts should give you some idea of what a frightful, killing drive this horse was put to. There is no counterpart of it in racing.

It shot him to the head of the pack—in the clear, and swinging for home. But now the real drive was on and the lightly-weighted Stagehand had come around horses and was thundering at his girth. At the eighth pole they were head and head.

As long as races are run they will be talking about that finish. One-eighth of a mile they flew, locked together. To the frenzied thousands it seemed impossible that Seabiscuit could last, but stick it he did, having been wide open for six furlongs. Head and head, nostril to nostril, stride for stride—out on his feet, he would not quit. And, as a year ago, when it was over no one knew the answer. The camera told the story—Stagehand by two and one-half inches.

It is one of the many things about him that stands alone in the record books—two nose defeats on consecutive years for the world's richest race—and neither defeat, in all honesty, his fault.

He came back to the stands, walking surely, his head still high, proud as Lucifer. To those who loved him, and they were legion, there was nothing more gallant and heart-breaking than that sight. They thought not of two great races lost, but of the individual who had lost them. The winner received an ovation—the loser a greater ovation. No tribute was ever finer for, remember, most of those people had bet on him and lost. For once the money didn't count, and therein lay a victory greater than the race itself.

Mrs. Howard and Red Pollard, way up on the roof, were crying like children. Charles and Tom were like frozen statues. Would he now ever win this race they had set their hearts on. He was five years old—next year he would be six, and the racing life of a horse is short at best. It just didn't seem in the cards. The odds against him were as high as the seamed Sierra Madres whose shadow lay in purple light over the racetrack.

They went down to him on the course, and they hadn't stood by him a minute before they were both smiling. He was as sturdy and strong and real as ever.

"We'll try again," Howard said, "and next time you'll win it."

But he was only saying it because something he saw in the horse made him say it—the look John Paul Jones had when the Bon Homme Richard was sinking and he shouted above the smoke of battle, "I haven't yet begun to fight!"

* * * *

On March 27th he was seen for one day at glamorous Agua Caliente, where he added his name to the long roster of famous horses who had won the handicap "south of the border." It was the only race he ever ran outside of the United States, and in winning it he added the echo of his hoofbeats to those of Phar Lap, Victorian, Mike Hall, and the others who had hallowed the ground of Baja California.

He journeyed northward again, and on April the 16th cracked another track record in winning the Bay Meadows Handicap. It was the first time he had carried as high as 133 pounds, but the excessive weight bothered him not at all and he won easily over Gosum and Today.

Meanwhile New York was clamoring for a match race with War Admiral. The old arguments pro and con had come to life with a bang—probably they had never died—and the Westchester Racing Association which operates Belmont Park—was offering a fabulous pot of $100,000, winner take all.

The Howards picked up the gauntlet and travelled east. The great commuter was on his way again. The race was to be run on Memorial Day, May the 30th, and the advance enthusiasm reached a peak never before attained on any racing event. At last the race of the century was to take place!

For once he did not ship well. The long grind—he had not been definitely out of training since March of 1936—had begun to tell on him. The iron nerves were taut, and the iron limbs were weary. He did not train well. His heart simply wasn't in it.

"I couldn't get him to work a mile better than 1:42, and that was driving him," Tom said.

He was beset with callers down at the Long Island course—photographers, newsmen, and thousands of the "just curious." One day a group came around asking for pictures. They had been at it all that day. The horse was feeding. Could they have him out of the stall? Tom tried to argue, but the strain was telling on his nerves, too.

"All right," he finally said, "I'll bring him out, but I'll bet any of you a thousand dollar bill that if I do there'll be no match race."

He brought him out, and there was no race—not for awhile, anyway. It was called off on the 24th of May. Seabiscuit's condition had gone from bad to worse. His knees were bothering him. There was even talk then that he was through for good. It was ill-advised and decidedly premature.

Howard stated to the press: "It was plain that to go on working him might endanger him permanently, so, with the consent of the Westchester Racing Association and the New York State Racing Commission, we decided to withdraw him from the special race."

They moved to Boston and with a short rest he came back to normality. His phenomenal constitution responded at once to a regime of absolute quiet and regularity. His works picked up, and it was felt that he would be ready to go in the Massachusetts Handicap on June 29th.

The jinx was riding high! The day of the race in his final blowout he rapped himself on the tendon of his left front leg. That left front again—he was building up for real trouble with it someday. Desperate measures were taken to remedy the situation, but, though a very temporary injury in itself, it was decided, on the advice of veterinarians, that to run him over the off condition of the track would be suicidal.

He was scratched shortly before post time, and loud were the wails and cat-calls attending that announcement. The good Bostonians, who had cheered him to the skies the year before when he won this same Massachusetts Handicap, now changed their tune to booing. He started west again under a cloud he hardly deserved. The old horse was breaking up, they said. He wasn't the same—the stable was afraid of War Admiral—he'd just be fading out of the picture now—too bad. . . . All that kind of talk was dished out in copious quantities.

The long westward trek was made to fulfill his engagement in the first running of the $50,000 added Hollywood Gold Cup, the premier offering of the beautiful new course at Inglewood, California. He broke the trip in Chicago to go

PIMLICO MATCH RACE—SEABISCUIT AND WAR ADMIRAL

Left: The start. Lower left: Turning for home. Below: The finish.

postward for the first time in that city in the Stars and Stripes Handicap. The Arlington Park racing strip on that July 4th day was deep in mud, but the Howards, not to disappoint the vast throng gathered to see the champion, sent him out in spite of the going. He ran second to War Minstrel, giving that horse, who the week before had finished ahead of War Admiral in the Massachusetts Handicap, twenty-three pounds.

The Gold Cup was twelve days and two thousand miles away. Off they went, with the long horse pullman cleared of all but Pumpkin and Seabiscuit and the latter's handlers. Hooked to the Santa Fe Chief the gleaming special car sped across plains and mountains—burning daylight and streaming darkness—onward to new conquests. At every stop Pumpkin was crowded into a far corner and Seabiscuit, Tom Smith at his head, was jogged up and down the length of the car.

"We had to keep him limbered up," Smith said. "The Cup race would be run only a few days after we landed. He took to it as easy as you please—Kansas City, Albuquerque—all those stops meant nothing to him but a chance to take a breeze around a pullman car."

Crowds gathered at the stations, peered in at the jogging bay horse. Who is it? Seabiscuit. The crowds grew. "Look, they've got Seabiscuit in there—the famous racehorse—yeah, that's him trotting up and down. Snooty lookin' little guy, ain't he? Kinda cute, though."

Pumpkin probably had a good horse laugh at that latter statement. "You're cute, little fella—did you hear 'em? Come on, keep jogging—it's good for you. Waltz me around again, Willie." Seabiscuit paid no attention. There was work to do—work and more work.

The crowds cheered as the long train rolled out of Kansas City. The wires tapped the message westward—Seabiscuit was coming. At Albuquerque the Indians looked in at the world's fastest horse and grunted approval. Looked like heap good cowpony. Rolling again, through New Mexico and Arizona, and down through the orange groves into California, and home.

So they'd thought he was all washed up back east, eh? Well, there was life in the old bones yet—he'd show 'em. First off, he'd show 'em in the Hollywood Gold Cup. One thing at a time. Let War Admiral wait.

Show 'em he did, and that before a vast crowd of forty thousand people. He went winging around those infield lakes to set a new track record, packing high weight of 133 pounds. His run down the stretch that day was something to write home about, for Specify, turning for home, was on top by eight lengths. Nothing daunted, the Biscuit flattened himself out and went to town, winning going away by one and one-half lengths. California gave her favorite son a deafening ovation. The jinx was behind him. The old knees were right again.

* * * *

One night in July, a few days after the Gold Cup, Bing Crosby telephoned his friend, Bill Quigley. Quigley was, and is, manager and vice-president of the little seaside course at Del Mar. Crosby is its president, and also operates a racing stable in partnership with Lin Howard, Charlie's son. The Binglin Stable they call it.

"Sounds like the name of a Chinese laundry," Crosby said, "but we've got a South American horse that can run away and hide from most of these local colts." He was right. The horse—Ligaroti—had already won three stakes at the Hollywood meeting, and had held a mile record in the Argentine before his importation. "How about a match race next month with Seabiscuit down at Del Mar?" he asked.

Lin Howard chimed in. It became a family affair. "We're game if Dad is," he said. "We'll show him something with this horse." Lin was training Ligaroti.

"What about it?" they asked Quigley.

The latter held off at first. He was not in favor of match races. However, the idea took hold, and the newspapers got wind of it. It sounded like a natural—North America against South America—father against son. The two younger men, in a friendly way, baited the older, and Charles took them up without much delay. Quigley finally consented and the match was arranged for the 12th of August. It was to be run over the mile and one-eighth distance for a purse of $25,000, winner take all. Seabiscuit was allotted 130 pounds and Ligaroti 115. One stipulation which the Del Mar management insisted upon was that no public money should be bet on the race.

On the afternoon of the match twenty thousand people packed the little course. Special trains ran from Los Angeles and San Diego, the highways were black with cars, yachts rode at anchor in the near-by bay, and fifteen planes dotted the track airport across the San Dieguito River. Excitement ran at fever pitch. All Hollywood turned out to back the movie-owned horse. They organized cheering sections and carried large Ligaroti banners. The day was exotic and torrid, and the race itself was titanic.

The rivalry, held in friendly check by owners and public, had unfortunately spread in a more dangerous vein to the riders. Their behavior marred what might otherwise have been one of the grandest sporting spectacles of all time. Seabiscuit and Ligaroti traveled the entire distance never more than a head apart—first one on top and then the other—the final issue in doubt until the very last stride of the race. Then it was that Seabiscuit got his head in front to win by that margin, once again breaking a track record.

The jockeys, who had interfered with each other in the run down the stretch, and who were equally to blame, were set down for the remainder of the meeting. It was strongly felt that their tactics would have in no way changed the result of the match, and it was just as strongly felt that those tactics could never take away from the magnificent exhibition given by both horses.

* * * *

Riding the rails again—and this time with blood in his eye. The War Admiral race was on, and the east was saying it would be War Admiral on the front end, and old Seabiscuit nowhere. Was that so . . . well, let 'em holler all they wanted now . . . talk was cheap. He'd answer the bugle at Pimlico on November the 1st, and maybe he'd make these experts take back a little.

The great race had at long last been arranged by Alfred Gwynne Vanderbilt, President of the Maryland Jockey Club. Both Mr. Riddle and Mr. Howard had agreed to the conditions. Nothing now, barring accident, could stand in the way of this classic event—one which the entire country admitted would establish the champion of champions.

In the conditions agreed to it seemed that the Howards had conceded the major points to the Riddles—the walk-up start, the distance of the race, and the amount of weight to be carried—120 pounds each. They had not, however, conceded the victory. No sir! Nor had the little bay horse. . . .

CHAPTER NINE « I THINK I'LL BUY TWO TICKETS »

NOVEMBER the 1st, and the sun was shining down on the historic old hilltop course of Pimlico, and waking Baltimore City to its greatest race day since Parole had conquered Ten Broeck and Tom Ochiltree back in 1877. There had been high revelry by night to the strains of "Maryland, my Maryland," and now the day of days had come.

And come, too, had the sporting gentry of a continent—from the north and south, and from the east and west. They had come to see the battle of the giants, and nine-tenths of them had come with money jingling in their jeans to bet on War Admiral's patrician nose. True, the west was there in force to back their darling, but the south and the eastern seaboard, almost to a man, went out on a limb for the Riddle colt. Ah, great was the sawing thereof—when that limb fell the noise was heard round the world!

Eight o'clock of the morning at trackside, and Jervis Spencer, chairman of the Maryland Racing Commission, joined Alfred Vanderbilt in the winner's circle. He had just completed an inspection tour of the racing oval, and now, smiling reassuringly at Vanderbilt, he stepped to the microphone made ready for this long awaited announcement:

"In my opinion the track will be fast this afternoon. The race is on!"

It had hinged on that statement. Both owners had agreed to run if Spencer pronounced the track condition favorable.

A cheer went up from the crowd of sports writers and turfmen gathered about the inclosure. Clem McCarthy took the mike and interviewed the experts.

"Whom do you like? Who'll win it?"

"War Admiral easy—War Admiral by two—the Admiral in a gallop."

Man after man went out on the limb. McCarthy looked over the crowd. The tanned face of the man from California was creased with a half smile. "What about it, Mr. Howard? You got anything to say?"

The smile broadened. Charles came forward and spoke into the mike.

"Clem," he said, "I was about to go and buy myself a ticket on Seabiscuit, but after hearing the opinions of all these experts—I think I'll buy two tickets."

They laughed good-naturedly. Poor fellow—he really thought that little horse of his could win it.

And up at the stable Seabiscuit stood quietly, waiting. He didn't think—he knew. Mrs. Howard came to the stall. His ears came up, alert, and he thrust his wide head toward her. She stroked him gently.

"This afternoon," she said, "you will carry on your saddle cloth the medal of Saint Christopher, patron saint of travelers."

He nodded once as though he understood.

Later, out on the racetrack, Howard met Jim Fitzsimmons—Sunny Jim, who had once had Seabiscuit in his barn.

"What do you think, Mr. Fitz?" he asked.

"I don't know what orders you and Smith are givin' the jock," Mr. Fitz answered, "but if they're the right ones, your horse will win."

THE FINISH

HOLLYWOOD GOLD CUP RACE

IN THE WINNER'S CIRCLE
Tom Smith, Anita Louise, Charles Howard

"We've already set those orders, but I'd like to hear if they agree with what you'd do."

"I'd tell the boy to take the track from him right at the start—go to the front and stay there."

"Just what we have told him," Howard said.

And, by heaven, just what he did!

Twice they came up to the flag, and twice turned back. George Woolf who rode him—poor Pollard was still crippled on the side-lines—was not to be caught napping in a walk-up flag start. The third time they were set—both horses nose and nose. The flag fell, and with it fell Woolf's whip—once, twice, and again.

A gasp of complete astonishment, of utter amazement, went up from the vast crowd. Two jumps and the little westerner was on top—ten jumps and he was coming away. He was leaving War Admiral—War Admiral, the fastest breaking horse in the world! He was leaving him flat-footed, beating him at his own game.

A half a length on top—a length—and, by the stands the first time, he had drawn out to a lead of two lengths. He had come down that long straightaway from the flag-fall like a shot out of a cannon. Around the clubhouse turn they swept, and now Woolf, the "ice-man," was sitting still, steadying him. The crowd was stunned into momentary silence.

On the backstretch Kurtsinger aboard the Admiral made his move, and the gallant Riddle horse, with a tremendous burst of speed, came abreast of Seabiscuit. The crowd roared—here it was—the Admiral would take him now—he'd go to the front. But he didn't. Woolf let out a rap in the reins, the Biscuit flattened a little lower, both ears pinned back.

Eye to eye, "going a mill-tail," they swung the far turn. The Admiral was all out and driving, but he couldn't pass the bay horse. At long last he had met his master, and when they turned for home all doubt on that point was removed forever. Moving with the precision and power of some magnificently tuned machine, Seabiscuit came grandly down to the wire, galloping away. The Riddle colt, game, gallant animal that he was, had given his all and found it not enough. He was simply staggering in the wake. Seabiscuit, by four open lengths, was champion of champions.

The crowd, who had treated him lightly before the race, suddenly awoke to the fact that they had seen one of the greatest horses of all time. Though most of them had lost money betting against him, they now surged down toward the racetrack, breaking police lines, climbing over the course rails, screaming and yelling like Comanche Indians on the warpath. Back through this bedlam of cheering, jostling, shouting people he came, sedately and calmly. Total strangers were leaning on his rump and his shoulders, patting him, pushing him, practically walking on him. He never batted an eye nor hurt a living soul. He had done his job, won the race, hung up another track record. Well, it was a day's work. Charlie and Tom were there, close by his head. In the gathering darkness up the track he could see the outline of the stable roof. There was a deep-bedded stall there, and dinner. And there wouldn't be any more of this silly talk about who was boss of the racetracks.

In the winner's circle he quietly reached around and nibbled at the wreath of flowers. Why miss a chance for a snack! The medal of Saint Christopher winked in the last rays of the sun.

CHAPTER TEN « A CHAMPION FALTERS »

"TOM, he looks grand—and a happy New Year to both of you."

The train hadn't even stopped yet, but Charles Howard was running alongside the slowing car, and Seabiscuit, his head thrust out the door, was blasting a salute to California sunshine and Santa Anita Park. The Dalmatian pup, Match, presented to him by admirers after the War Admiral race, frolicked about at the open door and would have taken a header if a groom hadn't grabbed his wagging tail. The Biscuit's new night watchman, the police dog Silver, was held back on a heavy leash. Even the placid Pumpkin awoke to the realization that they were home again—that this was January 1st of 1939. "Lafayette, we are here" —or words to that effect. "And you, little pal, will be trying again for that race that has dogged you so long. In the words of my Spanish ancestors," Pumpkin might have added, "via con Dios."

The train stopped and Pumpkin, as was his custom, led the way out onto the platform. Seabiscuit, Tom Smith holding the shank, followed. Howard was so excited that one of the horsemen in the reception crowd stated dryly, "They ought to put the lead-rope on him—he's a lot more nervous than the old horse."

Down the long loading platform he walked, and once his feet touched solid earth he let out another blast and flashed his heels to the sun.

"By golly," said a bystander, "look at the old devil! Six years old, eighty-four races run, $340,000 earned—and here he is again, back for more."

"Yeah," agreed his companion, "but them pins won't hold up forever. Now if he were mine. . . ."

But the horse wasn't his—fortunately he was Howard's and Smith's, and those two were fighters, like the Biscuit. They'd set a goal for him, and all three of them would keep on until that goal was reached.

Silver stood on his hind legs and tried to lick the horse's nose. Seabiscuit playfully nipped at the big dog. He reared and pawed the air with his front feet. "Out of my way, boys. Let's go to the barn—I'm hungry."

After four days and four nights of traveling from Columbia, South Carolina, via New Orleans, he was hungry. The entourage trailed him toward the red and white stable that had housed him so often—newsmen, cameramen, horsemen, onlookers. Probably they had all celebrated New Year's eve the night before, but then that occasion came every year. Most of them felt reasonably certain that this was the last time Seabiscuit would come back to Santa Anita.

* * * *

Rumors, which seem ever to dance attendance upon greatness, had come out of Columbia with annoying persistence—he wasn't training well, he wasn't training at all, the knees had finally given up the struggle, he was dead lame, he would never make the Santa Anita Handicap, he would never race again. Some green South Carolina reporter had looked goggle-eyed at his heavy night bandages and said to Tom Smith, "Gee, what's the matter with him?"

And Smith, fed up with rumors, but still with a twinkle in his eyes which escaped the reporter, answered, "Darn shame—but he broke both front legs."

Crazy as it sounds, modifications of the story spread. Those legs weren't busted everyone knew, but it was wondered if Tom weren't covering up for something else. Over three years in training—something must go wrong, even with an iron horse. The public refused to believe that he would ever reach Santa Anita until the day he arrived, and then they refused to believe he was sound.

The truth is, he had rapped that left front leg again while galloping down at Columbia—always that left front. And, as before, it was not serious at the time, but now Tom was worried. The knees would stand the long training grind, but would the oft injured leg? In his heart he knew the grand old campaigner needed a long rest. Smith was torn between two desires—go on and win that race which had been denied them twice, become the world's money-winning record holder, or let up with him now, play safe. A quality within the horse himself made the final decision for him. Seabiscuit had never played safe. Howard concurred, and galloping now in the face of danger, on they went.

There was something here one could not name—could not file away under any common heading. . . . Something perhaps written in the scroll of time long before any one of these three had been born.

* * * *

February 14th . . . Tuesday. . . . There's an old song they sing in the deep south:

If you put your money on a Tuesday's race,
You can see a smile on the horse's face.
"Go buy the crepe, old man," he'll say,
"For Tuesday is your Jonah day."

Maybe the crowd felt it. There was a hush over the stands that afternoon as the three-horse field broke from the gate—Seabiscuit, Today, and Marica. It was the Biscuit's first out since the great match race at Pimlico. The McCarthy color-bearer, Today, shot away from the post like a scared rabbit. He was under the light impost of 104 pounds, and it was plain from the first that he intended to make a runaway race of it if he could. Seabiscuit and the Taggart mare trailed close up down the backstretch. At the far turn Marica was done, and the Biscuit made his move, driving through on the rail to the McCarthy stallion's girth. They were flying now, going a pace where any bump was dangerous, and, according to the chart, both horses were momentarily in very close quarters. Suddenly, Today moved away, and the champion was seen to falter, almost to stumble. Something was wrong—no one knew what. His stride had been definitely checked. Two lengths he lost in a gasping fraction of time. Was he out of it? Had he broken down?

No, by George, he was coming on again, but he was not running evenly. Something *was* wrong! He lurched a little, he gave on the left side forward. Somehow he held his own down to the wire, struggling valiantly. He even gained a little on the winging leader, finishing two lengths behind him, with Marica up the racetrack in the dust. Today had broken the track record, traveling the mile in the blazing time of 1:35 and 3/5. Seabiscuit had given him 24 pounds.

Around the clubhouse turn George Woolf was standing in the irons, pulling him up. Thousands of eyes were riveted upon the horse. He was up in the bridle now, almost to a jog. Suddenly Woolf was seen to jump to the ground, run beside the Biscuit, stopping him. People were crowding down the ramp to the rail. Officials were walking up the track toward the champion. Tom Smith and Charles Howard were running.

Woolf turned him to come back, and he stood for a moment motionless. The turn had showed it beyond any shadow of doubt—the left front leg. The Biscuit was lame, badly lame. Painfully he

ROSEMONT AND SEABISCUIT

HANDICAP DAYS

STAGEHAND AND SEABISCUIT

walked back past the clubhouse. The crowds were shocked into complete silence. Gradually the silence broke in hoarse, strained whispers:

"He's through—he's broke down—look at that leg—poor old devil—the jinx again—he'll never win a Santa Anita Handicap now—they never come back—the king is dead. . . ."

But the king wasn't. His ankle and lower leg ached frightfully, and the pain shot clear to his shoulder. He was streaked with sweat, but his head went up when they stopped to blanket him, and he swung it proudly toward the gaping crowd. He liked them —he wanted them to like him, even broken and in defeat. And then again there was such a thing as morale, y'know—one didn't let down on parade—it simply wasn't done.

Somehow at the moment, more than ever in his life before, he stood for what all his breed had stood for. He represented family and background and blood. He was a direct challenge to those who, in any way, might ever have tried to infringe upon his rights to honesty and courage and dignity. He made a ridicule of all who had ever attempted to temporize with the reason for his, or any thoroughbred's birth. He stood as the guidon of decent living—of doing without fear or favor that which God had willed to be done—in his case, to run, be it on four legs or three—be it, if necessary, to crawl until his goal was reached.

Yes, he had come the last three-eighths of a mile practically on three legs. He was a thoroughbred, and in their creed it isn't so much what people know you will do, as the things they know you'll never do. You don't quit, and you don't show it when you are hurt.

They led him slowly away. The horse ambulance had come for him, but he had scorned it. He walked into the twilight, his stocky little figure finally disappearing in the gathering dusk. To those who watched him there was something both prophetic and final in that departure. He was, they said, leaving the racetrack forever.

Next day it was announced that he had ruptured a suspensory ligament. It was well-known that few horses were ever the same following such an injury. Shortly thereafter he was withdrawn from the Santa Anita Handicap list of nominations.

Now, they said, there could be no doubt of it—he was through —the old champion had run his last race—the jinx had been fulfilled.

But there were two men who didn't say it or think it—two men and one horse. . . .

CHAPTER ELEVEN «IN THE CALIFORNIA HILLS»

He was to be retired to the stud at Ridgewood, the northern California ranch of the Howards. He left Santa Anita in March. He was off to the tall timber, the land of mountains and pines and redwoods. He was to be a country boy now, to relax and rest those weary limbs, to let time give the final answer as to whether they might ever carry him to the racing wars again.

Horsemen, sportswriters, general public—they took it for granted that he would run no more. It was too bad he would never pass Sun Beau's money-winning record. He had ended up some $36,000 short of that goal. And it was too bad that he would never win a Santa Anita Handicap. The fates, they thought, had decreed otherwise.

So, in March of 1939, he came back to a farm for the first time since he had left Claiborne in the summer of 1934. Gingerly he walked out of the big van into the stable yard of Ridgewood. This was to be home eh . . . this pine-scented place far from the roaring crowds? He looked with amazement at the cows and chickens and pigs. Chickens he had seen—they had always appeared rather silly and nondescript. Cows and pigs were something new at close quarters. They didn't, frankly, look like they possessed much speed, and the latter got in your nose a bit. Still, he had always been tolerant.

The rim of the mountains seemed too close—a high, foreboding wall which shut out the world of galloping thunder he had left. There was still a job to do out there. He must hang on to that thought. He was homesick for the racetracks already. Where were Tom Smith and Pumpkin? Match and Silver? They could stay outside the mountain's rim, but he couldn't. Was that it? That fool leg of his—well, he'd show 'em. It felt better already. Just give him time. They thought they'd let that big black foreigner carry on for him, eh? What was his name? Kayak something? Second—Kayak second—that was it. That's where he'd be, too, if they ever met.

He was envious, he was lonely. It was all new and strange here in the big trees—and too quiet. Standing in the barnyard his ears were up, listening for the far sound of a bugle.

* * * *

He was unwound completely. He had long days of dozing in the paddock where the sunlight shone in patches on the grass. After the newness wore off he learned to tolerate the easy, humdrum regime of ranch life. It was as though he had made up his mind to it as a necessary interlude. He would not consider it more than that. Beyond those high hills the bugle was still blowing.

Across the fence and down the valley handsome mares were feeding. The sound of the racetrack bugle died away. He watched them with an interest new to him, but as old as life itself. His eyes grew deep with sudden fire, and the quiet valley echoed to the clarion call of a stallion. The mares looked up, moved forward beneath the trees. Again that challenge filled the amphitheater of the hills. Its echo was to go on and on, ringing down the vales of time, the challenge carried by his children, and his children's children.

He was mated to seven of those mares—Illeanna, Fair Knightess, Lucille K., Flying Belle, Lady Riaf, Sun Frolic, and Dressage. They were bred in the purple, those seven, daughters respectively of Polymelian, Bright Knight, Whiskalong, Flying Ebony, War Cry, Sun Briar, and Bull Dog.

He could not clearly see the future then. Had he been able to it would have pictured seven gangling youngsters following their proud mothers through the fields of Ridgewood within a few short weeks of the time their illustrious pappy was out in the world again, bringing home the bacon. The old slogan of "buy the baby shoes" held good—he did, and with a vengeance!

* * * *

The warm summer came to the northern California hills, and with it three old friends—the boss, Charles Howard; Mrs. Howard who was, he knew, a push-over for sugar and carrots and a few of those delicacies that his groom, Harry Bradshaw, had been hiding out on him lately; and the boy, Red Pollard, who had ridden him to so many of his great victories. Red had been out of the saddle, and in and out of hospitals for a long time. Fair Knightess had fallen with him and broken his collar bone, and then a green colt had gone down under him and crushed his leg. The leg had been broken again. Things had looked pretty black for Pollard. But Howard had seen him through his troubles, and a very charming young nurse had helped him back on his feet and married him. Today the picture was brightening for him. He was looking the Biscuit in the eye again.

"Just a couple of old cripples," Pollard said, his arm thrown lovingly about the horse's neck. He attempted a laugh, but it didn't have the same cock-sure ring of old. "We're all washed up, eh Pappy?"

"That's what they think outside." Howard pushed his sombrero back on his head. He looked from the carrot-topped boy to the great bay stallion. Both of them were out of condition—overweight, muscles softened, bones brittle. And yet. . . . He was not looking at them now, but beyond them.

Suddenly Pollard's body stiffened. He saw the light in Howard's eyes, and his own flashed.

"I get you, boss," he said slowly. "They think it outside, but—"

"But we don't, do we, Red?"

The jockey turned. His smile was as broad, as confident, as Howard's. He put out his hand and the older man took it in a strong grip.

"No sir—by golly, we don't—not now." The horse thrust his wide head between them. They both looked at him. "He never did believe it, Mr. Howard," Pollard added.

"Long ago in Detroit, Red, you told me we had the winner of the Santa Anita Handicap—you remember?"

"Yes sir."

"And I said, 'if that's so I guess a red-head better be riding him'." He paused. He straightened Seabiscuit's forelock, thoughtfully tapped the horse between the eyes. "It's been a long pull. We're none of us getting any younger." He was talking to the Biscuit now. "It's going to take weeks, months of exacting, relentless work. They're going to brand us as crazy, and there'll be times when we'll think they're pretty near right. But if we keep faith with ourselves and the good Lord—if we know in our hearts it can be done, then—then, by heaven, it can. What do you say, old-timer?"

The Biscuit's muzzle thrust hard against Howard's chest. The splendid head was tossed high, ears up, eyes focused far beyond the mountains. That post bugle was sounding again!

"He's just been marking time till the day came," Red said.

"The day has come," Howard answered. "What are we waiting for!"

* * * *

It was to be a long, relentless grind—Charles Howard had been right. Each step of that comeback trail must be planned and carried out with meticulous care. One false move might prove disastrous —undo everything which had gone before. They had no way of definitely knowing that his bad leg would stand training—in fact the odds were against it doing so. It was, in a way, like handling glass, and it was made the more difficult by the horse's very willingness to co-operate in the manner which he had decided was best. He was too full of life, too ready to run, too anxious to get the feel of a racetrack under him again.

Patience must be pounded into him. They were talking it to him, even as they must keep talking it to themselves. Go slowly, little hoss—take it easy. Those muscles must be hardened, those extra pounds taken off gradually. You get on your hind legs and try to light out now, and that added weight will bring back all your leg and knee trouble. Gently, Pappy—gently. Give yourself time—give Pollard time. He's on the long trail back, too. It's only July, Biscuit, and the Santa Anita Handicap is run in March. . . .

"Honestly, we held our breaths every time we took him out," Howard told me. "Tom Smith was east with Kayak, and it was up to Red and me. We made a track down on the floor of the valley. All we wanted to do was leg him up, get some of that fat off, and be able to turn over a sound horse to Tom when he came back in the fall."

That's just what they did do—and more power to them. It was a masterful job. Red was still weak, and the horse was full of the old Nick. The boy could not be turned loose on him for a moment. Every morning—week after week—Howard ponied them around that track, riding his pinto, Tick Tock, and keeping Seabiscuit back on a strong lead. At first they only walked him, later jogged him—a mile, two miles, three—gradually building him up.

It was nerve-wracking work. "At first the deer bothered him," Howard told me. "There were gullies and brush in the center of that field. They'd jump out of 'em and go winging off. Good Lord, the first time he spotted one he thought the race was on! Pollard swears to this day that he tried to imitate their funny, jumpy stride. But we stayed together in one piece and got him quieted down out of that."

Harry Bradshaw's work was on the ground, but it was just as exacting. Day and night he watched him, cut down his diet, muzzled him so he wouldn't eat his bedding. The whole ranch became centered in the one job—bring the Biscuit back. Even the pigs quit grunting at him and the chickens kept out of his way. He'd swing his head and stamp his feet and make a terrible racket hollering for food.

"At times it was pathetic—almost more than you could stand," Howard said, "but we didn't give in. We stuck to that diet, and the flesh came off and the muscles hardened."

Only one man on the ranch ever broke the rules. He couldn't take it, and he was caught slipping the old horse carrots when he thought the coast was clear. The axe fell—it had to. The whole chain was only as strong as its weakest link.

"He never knew a sick day on that comeback trail," Harry Bradshaw said. "We were all working for the same end, but we couldn't have ever done it if he hadn't been the horse that he is."

In November the big van rolled again into Ridgewood, and Seabiscuit, snorting good-bye at his barnyard friends, was on his way once more—out over the mountains into the world he knew and loved.

That world, which had considered his retirement permanent, now sat down over its morning coffee in amazement and skepticism to read the headlines: "Seabiscuit at Tanforan—In training again for 4th try at Santa Anita Handicap—Tom Smith returns from east to take charge of Seabiscuit's comeback—Old horse to make last attempt at money-winning record and world's richest race—Experts agree he has little chance of ever getting to the post—They don't come back. . . ."

No one mentioned that he was as sound as a bell of brass again, and that Tom Smith, after he had seen him gallop, said quietly to himself, "He was never better in his life."

The general comment over the breakfast coffee was, "Well, I simply couldn't watch him run. Why, the poor old dear would probably go to pieces like the one-horse shay!"

* * * *

Here we come again, Santa Anita!

In the last days of the year 1939 he moved once more upon the Colossus of Arcadia. This time there was more fanfare for Kayak's arrival than for Seabiscuit's. The public still had its tongue in its cheek, nor was it to remove it until the great day itself. Then, in its gulping wonder, it nearly swallowed it!

The stable was bluffing, they said. To be sure, handicapper Webb Everett had assigned him top weight of 130 pounds, and had rated both Kayak and Challedon below him. That, reasoned the fans, was only because he had once been great.

They may have overlooked a rather significant little move that Tom Smith made upon the Biscuit's arrival. He removed Kayak from the big double stall reserved for the stable's "head man," and led Seabiscuit into his old place at the top of the line. The king was dead, eh? Not in Tom's book. "Kayak never saw the day he could beat this horse," he once told me.

However, his works were not impressive. He was short, stated the experts—too fat, his wind couldn't be right after that long lay up. The bad leg would go—just wait and see.

That bad leg didn't go, and the knees were better than they had ever been. He was galloping freer, reaching out more. And they need not have worried too much about the wind. What had he taken those five mile canters for, if not that? Weight was a continual worry. The day after he arrived he tipped the scales at 1070 pounds, and his racing weight was 1040. Rubber hoods and long gallops cut it down.

Rain postponed his first appearance three times. They could take no chances with off track conditions now. Finally, on February 9th—just five days short of a year since his last race—he opened his 1940 campaign in a seven furlong sprint. He came out in four bandages, and the skeptics nodded. Giving 10 pounds to Heelfly and 13 to Sun Egret, he followed these two horses to the wire. Pollard was back in the saddle again and the crowd watched the "two old cripples" with fear and trembling. They didn't win, but they didn't end up in a heap on the racetrack either. As a matter of fact, they turned in a very creditable performance, Red keeping the horse out of trouble, and, once clear of it, sticking close to the leaders to the finish. Heelfly rolled the seven furlongs in 1:23 flat, and was loudly hailed after the running as the horse to beat in the Santa Anita Handicap. He was in that race with 114 pounds. It didn't look like Seabiscuit, off his present form, could give him 16 pounds and a beating.

So Heelfly got the huzzahs, and the Biscuit more sympathy, based upon the ever growing conviction that he was attempting the impossible. Howard and Smith said nothing. They were satisfied.

The public sympathy deepened after the San Carlos Handicap, run just eight days later. He did nothing in that to enhance his chances in the big race. He ran sixth, but again was in close quarters on the rail and Pollard had been forced to take him back and bide his time.

The wail was loud and long now. "Why don't they call it a day? Take the poor fellow out. He can never do it." There was a potent silence around the Howard barn. Two men and a horse had a job to do. The big race was but two weeks away.

Then came the San Antonio, the last prep before the $100,000 Handicap, and with it, like a hurricane blowing down the stretch, came the Seabiscuit of old—the champion of champions. Running his opposition dizzy he took the lead from Vino Puro as they swept out of the far turn, and from then on he was never in danger. He ran the mile and one-sixteenth in 1:42 and 2/5, equalling the track record set by his stablemate, Kayak II the year before. The latter, going as an entry with him, got up to be second, two full lengths back of the little bay horse.

It was impressive—it was magnificent. Here was the blazing speed of old, and here was the same red-headed, ridin' fool of old, too—Pollard and the Biscuit at their best. But, by all the saints, it didn't convince John Public! It was an odd mental set-up. Not only those who saw that San Antonio, but the sporting world at large, had made up its collective minds that it couldn't be done—that the old horse couldn't come back from retirement and win that race which had twice been denied him.

Their hopes and their prayers were with him, but deep inside them lay the conviction that he was still attempting the impossible. It had never been done—it couldn't be done now. They would have to see it to believe it.

See it they did!

CHAPTER TWELVE «IT CAN BE DONE»

THERE THEY GO! Like a great, breaking wave the horses roll away from the starting gate . . . straining bodies, flashing silks, flying hoofs. The hundred thousand dollar Santa Anita Handicap is on . . . the line of thoroughbreds streaming down the long stretch from the mile and one-quarter chute. They are driving for position in the first thundering flight before the clubhouse turn is reached.

Seventy-five thousand people are up now, yelling, struggling for vantage points, standing on chairs, swarming the ramps, balancing on other people's shoulders. The infield is milling with a vast sea of humanity, eddies and swirls of which flow about the entire circumference of the course. First turn, backstretch, far turn, and home stretch are black with people.

Howard and Smith in the box are trying to hold their field glasses steady. Sweat bobs from their eyebrows and blurs their eyes. "Drive him, Red, drive him. Get your position. Remember those other races. That's right—come on, boy. . . ." They are talking to themselves—praying.

Mrs. Howard had thought she couldn't watch it—she would stay at the stable—wait for him to come back. She is running now for the racetrack rail nearest the barn—it is way up in the chute. She is gasping for breath—shaking. She can't watch it—she can't see. But she's got to see—she's got to—it's his last race—win, lose, or draw, she's got to see it. Far away down the stretch the field is a hugh, brownish blot . . . a hundred legged bug scurrying over the earth. Desperately she climbs to the high seat of the track sprinkling wagon. Seabiscuit and Pollard—where are they? . . .

With a whirring roar the horses sweep by the stands and into the first turn. People are shouting: "He's up there! Look at him—the Biscuit—he's flying—he's right with the leaders—Pollard's using his head—he's watching the others. Thata boy, Red—move him—keep him clear. He's second now behind Whichcee—he's ridin' pretty. Let him roll, Red, let him roll! . . ."

A young lady is choking her escort. A man is pounding the derby hat of the person in front of him. A gentleman in the clubhouse has fallen off his chair into the ample lap of an old woman who is swearing softly because she can't see a thing. Bedlam has broken loose!

He's second, and they've straightened away on the backstretch. He's moving on Whichcee, but Red is sitting still. The horse under him is full of run. He's the Seabiscuit of old. Pollard knows that—feels it. And this time, by heaven, there isn't a field of horses to go around! He's right there—waiting to strike. Cool as ice—Red and the little bay thoroughbred. Today is the day . . . forget those other years. . . .

They're going into the far turn. Seabiscuit is lapped on Whichcee. Wedding Call and Royal Crusader are close now—dangerously close. Cluck to him, Red—move him, boy. Keep out of a jam. He's done it! He's done it! Royal Crusader is through—Wedding Call can't stay with the frightful pace. The Biscuit's killing 'em off—the old champion coming into his own. Heelfly is out of it, Kayak is moving from far back. Specify, War Plumage, Can't Wait, the two Argentines Don Mike and Ra 2nd—the burning speed has left them charred and gutted—they are nowhere. Whichcee is

TURN FOR HOM

still on the front end—staggering, dizzy. Seabiscuit is turning for home now, flying, running the greatest race of his life. He's galloping into a fury of sound, wave on wave of it beating out over the course until it seems that neither man nor beast would ever be able to move against it.

"Come on, Biscuit! Ride him, Red, ride him! He's going to the front—he's passing Whichcee. Let 'er roll, little hoss, let 'er roll! . . ."

The derby was pounded flat, the escort was choked half to death, the fat old lady was screaming instead of swearing, the air was filled with hats, programs, arms, roaring sound.

He has passed Whichcee—he is drawing away. Kayak is coming on the outside like a big black locomotive. He will never catch his stablemate. That goal, so long sought, so cruelly denied, is there now. Seabiscuit has rocketed past it, a length and a half on top. He has won the Santa Anita Handicap—no camera needed for this one! He has, with 130 pounds up, set a new track record of 2:01 and 1/5—the second fastest mile and one-quarter ever run in American history. He has passed Sun Beau's money mark by over $60,000, for he has earned over that long trail $437,730—the little runt who had once been entered in a claiming race for $2,500.

He was old, was he? Broken down? Champions don't come back, eh? Tell that to the Marines! Here's one that did. Here's one that stands alone through the years, the symbol of greatness, of courage, of honest endeavor . . . one whose hoofbeats will echo in the hallowed halls of time till the last post bugle has sounded, and great horses gallop no more on this earth.

He is in the winner's circle, the wreath of flowers draped over his broad shoulders, Red Pollard on his back. Howard and Smith are beside him. Far up the track by the stable Mrs. Howard is still sitting on the high seat of the wagon, too weak, too thankful now that it is over, to move. Her field glasses, unnoticed, have dropped from her nerveless hands to the dust below.

There are five people closest to this picture—Seabiscuit, Charles Howard, his wife, Red Pollard, and Tom Smith. They have all won. And yet, in a sense, there are countless millions of others who have won . . . who have found the world a little bit better place to live in because of a great horse. . . . It is not so much what he has done in life that counts—the victories, the glorious defeats, the fabulous money earned. It is, in the final analysis, the kindly, courageous, honest manner in which he has lived. . . . Thus will the fine flame of his soul burn in the tunnel of time forever. . . .

THE WINNER'S CIRCLE FO
THE GREAT CHAMPION